BRISTOL

"The most beautiful, interesting and distinguished city in England."

VIRTUTE ET INDUSTRIA

A history

compiled, edited and written
by

Peter Macdonald

Petmac Publications, Bristol

Second Edition.

Cover picture "Home for Christmas" by Eric Bottomley G.R.A., 1992

ISBN 0 9527009 1 3

Printed by J.W.Arrowsmith, Ltd, Bristol

Petmac Publications, c/o J.W.Arrowsmith Ltd, Winterstoke Road, Bristol BS3 2NT

"To know of past times and of the places on the earth is both ornament and nutriment to the human mind."

Leonardo da Vinci

Bristol is not the oldest city in the nation but it is the most beautiful. It has not been the home of the greatest historical figures in the land but many great people have been born and lived here. It was never the most important port in England, but for a time only London had more ships and handled bigger tonnages. It pioneered trade in products from the New World and even played a major part in discovering that such a place existed. In being at one time the fountainhead of sherry and the biggest packager of tobacco in Britain it gave temporary oblivion to some and quietened the nerves of a lot more. Today, less sherry is imported, fewer cigarettes are made. Times change, but we, as a nation, still eat more chocolate per head of population than any other country in the world - Bristol has played its part in creating the gigantic waistlines of the panting ladies we see wheeling overflowing trolleys around our supermarkets.

These days Bristol produces planes, missiles, aero engines and computers and their software. It has become one of the greatest financial centres in the nation, with many major companies having moved into the city. Its nearby docks import a quarter of a million cars a year. It is the home of creative television and of progressive art. It thrives still, and long may it do so.

Now read on. It's a fascinating story.

1

"Bristol" was not called that until the 11th Century, and even then some people still referred to it as Bricg-stowe, or Brightstowe, which meant "the place of the bridge." From the earliest days of human habitation there has been a bridge over the Avon at what in time was to become the centre of this great city.

An Opinion of Bristol

"I feel that the people here enjoy life. There is not that terrible dreariness which is probably the chief curse of our provincial towns. It is a genuine city, an ancient metropolis. Bristol lives on, selling us Gold Flake and Fry's chocolate and soap and clothes and a hundred other things. And the smoke from a million Gold Flakes solidifies into a new Gothic tower for the university; and the chocolate melts away only to leave behind it all the fine shops down Park street, and the pleasant villas out at Clifton, and an occasional glass of Harvey's Bristol Milk for everyone."

J. B. Priestley, author and playwright, in **1933**:

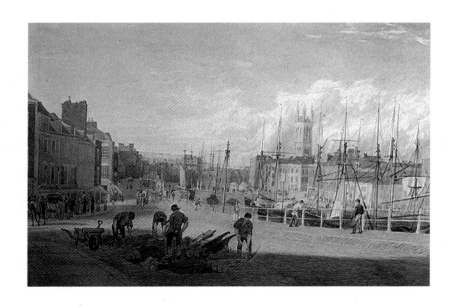

The Land and the First Settlements

The river Avon and one of its tributaries, the Trym, seem to defy natural laws. Both refuse to take the natural way to the sea, and instead of following the lower ground break through great masses of limestone, carving remarkable gorges for themselves in the process.

Before the Avon came into existence, the old rocks of the district evolved. Underneath lay sandstone, on the surface of which had been deposited a thick layer of limestone. Then came a period of tremendous volcanic upheaval; rocks were pushed up in the centre, forming an "upfold"; the surface of the upfold was subjected to the denuding action of rain, wind, and temperature, and was gradually carried away.

It was at this period that the Avon had its birth and established its present course. What climatic conditions existed here at that far-off time in the world's story it is difficult to imagine, but it is certain that the Avon was then not a slow-moving tidal stream but a torrent rushing at great speed to the sea. The river was well established and could not be turned aside by the outcrop of limestone that lay across its path; it cut away at its bed, deeper and deeper, while the hard rock on either side resisted the weathering action of rain and wind. Thus was formed the beautiful Avon gorge... [1]

Penpark Hole

A few miles away to the north of the gorge another fault in the rock became what is known as Pen Park Hole. The second deepest cavern in England, it lies under what is now Southmead, the entrances blocked off with concrete since the 1960s.

The cleric with the enquiring mind

"*Thou hast laid me in the lowest pit, in a place of darkness and in the deep*," was the psalm for morning service in Clifton Parish church on a Spring morning in 1755. The clear voice of the young canon helping in the service carried resonantly round the church and two young ladies at the back of the church agreed that he really was quite handsome. They were looking forward to the adventure that awaited them after the service, for Tom Newnham, 26-year-old minor canon at Bristol cathedral, had asked them to make up a foursome to go exploring Hell's Kitchen.

Arriving at the fields where Pen Park Road now runs, the four young people walked to where a big ash tree marked the main entrance to the Hole. Tom Newnham planned to measure the depths of the cavern, said to be 200 feet deep. He had brought with him a ball of twine weighted at one end and aimed to swing the line down the main entrance and see how far it would reach. Watched by his friends the young cleric scrambled down the incline leading towards the entrance to the shaft. To steady himself he reached up and held on the branch of the ash tree. Then, like an energetic angler casting a line, he flung the twine down the shaft. There was an ominous crack - the branch on which his full weight now depended was breaking. He made a desperate attempt to save himself, tried to gain a foothold, but the ground was wet from a recent shower. The branch snapped, and before the horrified gaze of his friends he plunged down the shaft and vanished from sight. They ran to get help, but there was no hope. It took many days of searching before his body was found floating in the subterranean water. While the search went on big crowds came to the scene, many of them picnicking to while away the time.

And the soldier who went down the hole

Seventy-three years before, in 1682, another man had become a victim of the hole when Captain Sturmy and a companion descended on ropes, using candles for illumination, to see if there was a possibility of lead being mined there, the shaft having been used, so they believed, for that purpose in medieval times. Some 220 feet down Sturmy and his friend saw what the captain later described as " a great hollow in the rock" above their heads. His companion climbed up to explore the hollow, walked seventy paces then returned much faster than he had gone, exclaiming that he had seen an evil spirit!

The story of the ghost was widely circulated when, a few days later, Sturmy took to his bed with a fever and died. [2]

Meanwhile, on the other side of Europe...

How Alexander the Great Met His Fate

At the hotel Openora,
In the northern part of Greece,
I studied local history
And this tale I will relate.

We'd received so many warnings
Of the mad dogs on the beach
And the many broken bottles
That the dustman could not reach

But the worst was of the buzzers
That fly about by night
Yes, those nasty little buzzards,
Blood suckers when they bite.

You know of Alexander,
He was born not far away
At the ancient site of Pella
Within the month of May.

It's known he died a young man,
As young men then did go,
But what he really died of,
Not many people know.

He'd conquered all of Persia
And almost half the world
But a simple fate did beat him,
As this story will unfurl.

Dallying with a duchess,
On the palace balcony,
Aiming to make corrections
To his barren family tree

He was bit in many places.
In the warm and pleasant air
He did not wear his braces
So his bottom was all bare.

Mosquitoes zoomed around him
And attacked him without fear
Though the fact he wore his helmet
Protected his left ear.

After dallying with the duchess
He scratched and scratched galore
And due to all this scratching
Became immensely sore.

And so died Alexander,
A warrior born and bred,
Eaten by mosquitoes
While in his lady's bed.

Peter C. Mitchell,
Southmead, Bristol, 1986

5

Pre-Roman Bristol

A quarter of a million years ago men made their homes in the valley of the Avon and used caves at Burrington and Cheddar for shelter. Three thousand years ago there was an Iron Age fort at Blaise. Pre-historic finds have been made in the mud of the Cumberland Basin, the Floating Harbour and the river Avon. A bone-handled Iron Age, or Celtic, weaving comb was unearthed near Baldwin Street and a tree-trunk, hollowed like a canoe, near St. Stephen's, in the City.

Before the Roman occupation the Bristol area was well-wooded, and sparsely populated by tribes who were nearly always at war with each other. They found refuge on high ground in circular earthworks topped with stone walls or wooden palisades. The cliffs on either side of the Avon gorge were ideal sites from which to command the low-water ford across the river which then existed almost under the present Suspension Bridge and one of their camps can be traced near the Observatory Tower, which stands inside the earthwork. It is thought that the Romans also used it hundreds of years later.

The Romans

The Romans made their headquarters in Britain in London, and as they proceeded with the conquest of the country followed their usual practice of linking up towns with roads that radiated outwards in almost straight lines.

A major road ran from London to Aqua Sulis (Bath), where there was a junction with the Fosse Way coming down from Lincoln. An extension of the West road was made from Bath to Abona, known to us as Sea Mills, from where troops and supplies [for the garrisons in South Wales] could quickly be ferried across the Severn.

A number of coins and other articles discovered at Abona may be seen in the Bristol museum. The remains of a villa have been unearthed near the railway station at Sea Mills. [The foundations are preserved by the side of the Portway.] Other villas have been discovered near Observatory Hill, at Winchester Road Brislington, and at Somerdale. (3)

There is little evidence of Roman settlement in Bristol but one of their main roads connecting Bath with Sea Mills ran through the town. It probably went through Hanham, St. George, over the Frome to Cold Harbour Road and then across Durdham Down and through Stoke Bishop to Sea Mills.

Part of the Roman road runs across the Downs near what is now known as Pitch and Pay Lane (in Sneyd Park), so named during a visitation of the plague. To avoid close contact and the risk of being infected, traders from the countryside threw their produce over a low fence to buyers from the city, who picked up the goods and threw the money they owed back over the fence. (If they didn't, there wasn't much the traders could do about it, was there?)

In 1969-70 during construction of the M5 motorway through Gloucestershire, archaeologists identified thirty previously unknown Roman villas. There are probably several more in the Bristol area.

> **There twice a day the Severn fills;**
> **The salt sea-water passes by,**
> **And hushes half the babbling Wye**
> **And makes a silence in the hills.**
>
> **Tennyson, *In Memorium***

Danes and then Normans

When the Romans left early in the 5th Century AD, Angles, Saxons and Jutes invaded England, spreading to the West. In the 8th and 9th Centuries they were in their turn attacked by marauding bands of Danes. The Bristol area lay on the fringe [of their advance], and therefore played little part in the main stream of events.

If Bristol was large enough to have a mint of its own in the time of Ethelred (**978**), as it had, then it had certainly been in existence for a considerable time. Yet it is fairly certain that no town existed in the year 577: "In this year," says the English Chronicle, " Cuthwine and Ceawlin fought against the Britons, and slew three kings...at the place called Deorham, and took three cities from them; Gloucester, Cirencester and Bath." If Bristol had been in existence at that time it would almost certainly have been mentioned, but as it was not, then we may assume that the town must have grown somewhere between 577 and 978 AD, when the earliest relic to have been found - a coin bearing the image of Ethelred the Unready - was minted.[3] Four or five pennies of the Danish-born King Cnut (Canute, who ruled England from 1016-1035) that were coined in Bristol still exist.

King Alfred saved the West from complete conquest by building ships to attack the Danes at sea and by encouraging his people to build fortified towns. It is very probable that Bristol was one of the towns founded at about the time of Alfred the Great (871-899).

The importance of the city in the 10th century is shown by the building of a second city wall. That there was a wall as early as **920** AD appears from chronicles, which attributed the first to the time of King Arthur, in the 6th Century. [4] [In other words, nobody really knows.]

By the time of the Norman Conquest a small town, port and market was already established. Bristol was sited in a well-defended position, above the point where the river Frome joined the Avon and where the two rivers provided a good anchorage for ships; well inland from the sea, safe from storms and pirates. By the year AD **1OOO** Bristol's inhabitants were engaged in overseas trade, mostly with Ireland.

"In the vale is the most celebrated town called Bristol, a port which is a commodious and safe harbour for all vessels, into which come ships from Ireland and Norway and other lands beyond the seas."

William of Malmesbury, 1125

1066 and all that

The first visitors to Bristol who left any real account of the town were the Commissioners sent by William the Conqueror as part of the enormous task of compiling the Domesday Survey of **1086**...This is how they described it in the terse and technical Latin of the Survey:

In Barton at Bristol were six hides. In demesne three curucates and 22 villeins and 25 bordars with 25 plough-teams. There are 10 serfs and 18 co-liberts having 14 plough-teams. There are 2 mills worth 140 shillings. He found here 2 hides and 2 plough-teams in demesne, and 17 villeins and 24 bordars with 21 plough-teams. There were 4 serfs and 3 co-liberts with 3 plough-teams. Of this land, the Church of Bristol holds three hides and has there one plough-team... and so on...[3]

At the time of the Conquest, Bristol was extremely small, divided into four wards by streets that still exist: Wine Street, Broad Street, Corn Street and High Street. The centre, where public meetings were held, proclamations read out and felons hanged was The Cross, where those roads met.

The city paid a rent to the king of £85 per annum.

After the Norman Conquest

Soon after the Conquest, Bristol castle was built by Bishop Geoffrey of Coutance. The castle towered over the town and stood on ground near to St. Peter's Church, extending across to the Broad Weir and the Old Market. It was divided into two parts, an Inner Ward and an Outer Ward. Within the Inner Ward was the little Chapel of St. Martin, standing on land known as Castle Green, and the lovely dining hall, a part of which can be seen near Tower Street. The hall was 36 yards long and contained the Knight's Table, a slab of marble 15ft in length. Rich and royal prisoners as well as the Reeve, or Lord of the Castle, lived in the Inner Ward. The Outer Ward contained the great well and the dungeons, besides apartments for the garrison. Encircling the Castle was a moat.

Artist's impression of what Bristol Castle looked like in its heyday

At the furthest end of the Inner Ward was the old Market, to which country folk came, through the Lawfords Gate, from the villages in the King's Wood to sell their produce at the Market Cross. Close by was the Castle orchard.

When Henry I died in **1135** his nephew Stephen became king. His reign was so chaotic that a common saying was "Christ and His saints are sleeping." Robert, Earl of Gloucester, one of the first occupants of Bristol castle, championed the cause of his half-sister, Maud, in her claim, as daughter of Henry I, to the English throne, thus making Bristol the headquarters of her party. In it gathered a band of mercenary soldiers, "**robbers and freebooters that appear not only terrible to onlookers but are truly horrible. They leave the castle to commit whatever pleases them,**" wrote a chronicler. They attacked Bath; seized rich men and cast them into the dungeons of the castle until they ransomed themselves with huge fines.

This lawless state of affairs gave Bristol merchants the opportunity to increase their notorious traffic in slaves, selling kidnapped young men and women, and even children, to a pagan race called Ostmen in Ireland. Slaves were valuable merchandise: a man was worth six oxen. Some parents sold off their sons and daughters and as time passed Bristol became known as The Stepmother of all England. (6)

BRISTOL CATHEDRAL,
THE NORMAN CHAPTER HOUSE.   43525.

11

Bristol Cathedral

An Augustinian abbey was founded beside College Green in **1140** by Robert Fitzharding, a Bristolian who later became Lord Berkeley. Income from lands owned by the abbey in Somerset and Gloucestershire enabled the friars to enlarge the original church during the Middle Ages, though work was badly affected by the Black Death of 1348, which killed up to 40 per cent of the population. Monks suffered acutely, and some monasteries never recovered; the abbey did, and by the early 16th Century the north transept and the central tower had been built and work began on rebuilding the original nave. When Henry VIII ordered the disbandment of the monasteries in 1539 the Augustinians departed and work ceased. In 1542 Bristol was one of six dioceses founded by the king, and the abbey became a cathedral - but for years it was only half a cathedral: for the next three centuries houses occupied the site of the former nave; by the early 19th Century some of them had become "a Receptacle for Prostitutes", and in 1838 they were demolished. In 1860 work began on rebuilding the cathedral as we now know it.

But piety, as is sometimes the case, was hypocritical...

"And yet, in a town called Bristol, opposite to Ireland, into which its inhabitants make frequent voyages on account of trade, Wulfstan cured the people of a most odious and inveterate custom of buying men and women in all parts of England and exporting them to Ireland for the sake of gain. You might have seen, with sorrow, long ranks of young persons of both sexes, and of the greatest beauty, tied together with ropes, and daily exposed to sale. Oh ! horrid wickedness ! to give up their nearest relations, nay, their own children, to slavery. Wulfstan made so great an impression on their minds that they abandoned that wicked trade."

So wrote a chronicler of the early 13th Century. Unfortunately, the people of Bristol had a change of heart, and it was some time after this that the practice ceased.

Bristol Cathedral School

The cathedral school was established between **1154** and **1171**. It is not known when boy choristers first began to sing beside College Green but many abbeys had choirs by the 14th Century. The School song celebrates Henry VIII's foundation of it after the Dissolution of the Monasteries.

When bluff King Hal had leisure
From matrimonial joys,
He took peculiar pleasure
In educating boys.
By Severn-side and Avon's tide,
By Isis, Dee and Nene,
He founded Schools (complete with rules)
To make good Englishmen.

Our old grey Abbey Mother
On all her sons looks down
And offers each new brother
Her golden three-fold crown:
A crown for him who's good of limb
A crown for love of learning
A crown apart for every heart
Where God's own fire is burning.

Here, where in lazier ages,
The fat Black Canons dined,
We masticate the pages
That feed the growing mind.
But, as we learn our bread to earn,
And play our varied parts,
Like distant drums the whisper comes
"Lift up, lift up your hearts!"

Her proud storm-beaten beauty
To all her children cries:
"Do more than just your duty
Be GREAT and win the prize!"
God grant us each some goal to reach
Of triple-crowned endeavour,
And make his school a vestibule
To his own courts for ever!

*

Chorus:
But of all the Schools that nestle
Beneath Cathedral towers,
The best School's the West School
The best School is ours!

13

The first lords and masters in this land,
And the chief towns first they let arrear,were
London and Lyncolne, and Leycestre;
Colchestre, Canterbyre, Brystoe and Worcestre.

Robert, the Rhyming Monk, 1200

THE LORD MAYOR'S CHAPEL

On the north side of College Green, facing the Cathedral, stands the beautiful Chapel of St. Mark, the only remains of the mediaeval Hospital of the Gaunts, founded shortly before his death in **1230** by Maurice de Gaunt. The south aisle was added about 1270. Later additions began at the end the 15th Century when, in 1487, the tower was built, followed by the Poyntz chapel in 1523, erected as a chantry by Sir Robert Poyntz of Iron Acton. He was a friend of both Henry VII and Henry VIII, died in 1520 and was buried in the chantry.

At the Dissolution of the Monasteries (1539), the hospital was surrendered to the commissioners appointed by the King. Two years later the property was sold to the Corporation of Bristol for £1,000. They adopted it, and as a result Bristol is the only city in the kingdom which has a chapel which is the exclusive property of the commonalty. Since 1722 the Corporation have used it as their official place of worship.[7]

Beside the Lord Mayor's seat is a magnificent sword rest which bears the initials "A.R.", for Anna Regina. It has sockets for the silver maces carried by policemen when they provide an escort for the Lord mayor, and a place for "Ye Cappe of Maintenance" worn by the Swordbearer (a fur hat made from Russian sable) on ceremonial occasions.

In the 12th and 13th Centuries "College Green appears to have been the place of burial belonging to the monastery of St Augustine and to the house of Gaunts, now the Lord Mayor's chapel. It was originally of considerable extent, bounded on one side by Frog Lane and containing in this direction two hundred and forty steps. Its greatest length was three hundred and sixty steps. Like all churchyards... it was a sanctuary."[8] But by the 17th Century visitors described College Green as having "many shady trees, and most delightful walkes, about which stands many stately buildings wherein many Gentlemen and Gentlewomen of note and rank doe live."

Dire Death of a King

The city played an important part in the conflicts between the barons and the Crown during the troubled reign of Edward II. In **1327** he was imprisoned in Bristol castle by his queen, Isabella, and her lover, Mortimer; later he was moved to Berkeley castle, where he was hideously murdered on 21st September, an incident commemorated in horrific detail by one of the roof-bosses in the north transcept of Bristol cathedral. [**A red-hot poker was poked where no poker should be poked. It is said his screams could be heard half a mile away. Yet how peaceful the place is today, with its long views towards the Severn Estuary. Nearby is the house in which Edward Jenner lived, the doctor who invented the smallpox vaccine that eliminated one of humanity's foulest diseases.**]

King Edward's body was refused burial at the abbey church of St Augustine - which was to become Bristol cathedral - and was interred in Gloucester Abbey. [3]

Common seal of the burgesses of Bristol

The Swordbearer

There has been a Swordbearer in Bristol since **1373**.

Among the city's treasures are four processional swords, the oldest of which is the Mourning Sword, made in the late 14th Century, probably during the reign of Edward III. It is carried in procession only on the occasion of ceremonies marking the death of the monarch, or the death of the Lord Mayor in office. The Pearl Sword is about as old. It is carried on Legal Sunday, when the judges go in procession to the cathedral, and Rush Sunday, when the Corporation attend St Mary Redcliffe. The third, the Lent sword, is not much younger: it was made in the early-15th Century and is carried on all formal occasions, such as the opening of the monthly Council meetings, Mayor-making and during the Armistice Day parade. The fourth sword is the State Sword, made in 1752. It is ornate, beautifully emblazoned with gold on a scarlet scabbard but is too large to be carried in procession. These days it is hung on the wall behind the Lord Mayor in the Council chamber during Council meetings. The Lent Sword was once used in anger, so it is said, when the Mayor was attacked by footpads as he walked across College Green and the Swordbearer defended him with it and put the muggers to flight.

Did You Know That

in **1340** Thomas **Blanket**, a wool trader of Bristol, became the first man to make blankets?

Majestic Bristol! to thy happy port
Prolific commerce makes its lov'd resort;
Thy gallant ships, with spacious sails, unfurl'd,
Waft, to thy shore, the treasures of the world!
With each production of the East and West,
Thy favor'd citizens are amply blest;
Thy active sons, unceasingly are sway'd
By honor, justice and a thirst for trade.[9]

16

The Plague

An unwelcome visitor came to Bristol in **1348**: the Black Death, which arrived in England at the Dorset port of Melcombe Regis in the summer of 1348 and spread rapidly northwards, reaching Bristol by the autumn. That year, Henry Knighton, a monk from Leicester, recorded in his Latin Chronicle:

"Then the dreadful pestilence ... came to Bristol, and there died almost all the strength of the town, suddenly overwhelmed by death, for there were few who were sick for more than three days, or two days, or even half a day. [Sometimes, people died between one step and the next.] Then this cruel death spread everywhere, following the course of the sun."

The death-rate among the clergy in Somerset during the plague of nearly 48 per cent. In Bristol, in the foul crowded dwellings of the poor, the toll was no doubt a great deal higher. The grass is said to have grown several inches high in Broad Street for want of an able-bodied man to cut it...

and, as if that wasn't enough to contend with there was...

FIRE,

an ever present threat in the old walled city of Bristol, where houses were tinder boxes of wood, and fire-fighting equipment non-existent. For this reason all house fires had to be extinguished when the bells of St Nicholas church sounded the curfew at 9 pm.

One of the most destructive fires occurred in **1647**, when flames swept across the timber houses on Bristol bridge, destroying twenty-four of them. As a result, the town council ordered a fire engine from London (cost £31 10s) plus 48 buckets (£8. 8s.). Each member of the council was required to keep six buckets in his house. [What did they use them for, I wonder? I hate to think.]

The Charter

In **1373,** when Edward III was in desperate need of money to pay for part of the Hundred Years War against France, 600 marks paid by the Corporation to the Crown secured Bristol a Charter granting it the status of an independent county; the first provincial town to be so honoured.

8th August, 47 Edward III, (1373)

Edward, by the grace of God, King of England and France and Lord of Ireland, to Archbishops, Bishops, Abbots, Priors, Dukes, Earls, Barons, Justices, Sheriffs, Reeves, Bailiffs, Ministers and all other his faithful people, greeting...

Know ye that whereas divers liberties and quittances have been granted for ever to our beloved burgesses of our town of Bristol and their heirs and successors . . we, at the supplications of our beloved Mayor and commonalty of the town aforesaid, have granted by this our charter ...that the said town of Bristol withall be a County by itself and called the County of Bristol for ever."

The Account of Nicholas Fermbaud, constable of Bristol castle

From Michaelmas at the end of the 28th year till Michaelmas at the end of the 31st year (AD 1300-1303):-

Receipts

£18.12s.10d. from prise of beer; 6d. rent from John of Woodstock; £1 from the produce of Peter Goldsmith's former garden; 15s. from Christine the clerk's and 13s.4d. from the king's garden outside the castle; **13.s from the rented schools of the Jews**; 6s. from the house in Wine St. which belonged to Cresse, the son of Isaac; nothing from the house which belonged to Moses of Kent; 3s.4d. from the farm of the former Jewish cemetery; 5s. from the house which belonged to Benedict of Winchester; **£24.3s.9½d from assessed rents in the hamlets of Stapleton, Mangotsfield and Easton; £1.1s** from grass/earth, etc. etc.

Sum of the receipt . . . **£134.8s.7½d.** **Nothing left in the treasury.** [So, what's new!]

Expenditure

£57.15s.10d. by the king's writ to Richard Siward knight, junior, to John de la More, John de Clogher, and John, son of Alexander of Moray, esquires, **prisoners from Scotland taken in the fight at Dunbar and staying in the castle,** also to their 2 keepers for wages; also £5.4s.8d. to Alexander Comyn, knight, similarly captured and confined, as **wages** until he was freed. Also £4.5s. to **Robert le Graunt esquire, a prisoner from Scotland taken in the same fight, as his wages staying in the castle.** £4.7s.3d. similarly to John de Moreue, who **died in prison**; £3.9s.4d. for Richard Siward junior, knight; **£1.7s. for 1 horse hired to take him from Bristol to Banstead and for the wages of 2 grooms escorting him there, for 11 days going and returning.**(10)

St Mary Redcliffe

"The length of the whole church of St Mary Redcliffe, except Lady Chapel, is 63 yards. The length of the Lady Chapel is 13 yards 1 1/2 feet, and its breadth 7 yards; the breadth of the whole church is 18 yards, the total length of Redcliffe church is 77 yards. The tower of St Mary Redcliffe is 300 feet high, of which 100 feet have been cast down by lightening".

William Wycestre, **1415-1485**?

The original intention was that the South porch should equal the splendour of the North porch, but instead it was built in a much less ornate manner because the Black Death came and most of the stone masons died.

Standing proudly on the little ridge whose exposed, red rock face gives the area its name, St. Mary Redcliffe is, as Queen Elizabeth I said in **1574, the** "finest, goodliest and most famous parish church in England". [Or did she? A recent book disputes the fact that she ever said it. Anyway, it would be nice to think that she had. If not, then she should have!]

Originally a twelfth-century chapel of ease in the large parish of Bedminster, it was mostly rebuilt at various times in the 14th Century. With its double-aisled transepts, its magnificent stone vaults and its eastern Lady chapel it gives the impression of a moderate-sized abbey church or a small cathedral. Much of its tall spire fell down in 1445, but was rebuilt, in the 1870s, to its original height of about 300 feet.[13]

In amongst its tapering columns is a memorial to Admiral Sir William Penn, father of the founder of Pennsylvania.

"*Forming a port fit and safe for a thousand vessels, Bristol's walls bind the circuit of the city so nearly and so closely that the whole city seems to swim on the water and be set on the river banks.*" The writer of the *Gesta Stephani* in **1141**.[4]

Revelry

Processions were a commonplace of urban life in the Middle Ages and the members of the Bristol city council attended many public functions in this fashion, each man in his scarlet robe walking in the place appropriate to his rank and seniority. In general, these processions had a double social meaning. Most obviously, they expressed in visible form the organisation of the municipal government; the persons holding each of the principal offices were publicly advertised. Not only were observers made aware of the hierarchy of power within the city, they were reminded through this symbolic expression of political authority of their own proper position in the community, and of the need to show deference to its leaders.

When they had all assembled on College Green there were "drynkyngs of sondry wines", and "Spysid Cakebrede" was eaten by the assembled celebrants. At the Hall the mayor and his brethren became the guests of the weavers, which gave the latter the opportunity to display their wealth and manifest their importance. Moreover, "the cuppes" were "merelly filled aboute the hous," which signifies the drinking of "healths" among the participants. Suitably inebriated, the council membership found their way "every man home" alone. What had started as an orderly procession now became a leaderless and unorganised - and disorderly - movement away from it. [So, again, what's new?]

At Corpus Christi. . .the members of every guild . . . assembled with music, flags and banners to join in a splendid ecclesiastical Procession through the streets, where houses were decorated with tapestry, brilliant cloth, and garlands of flowers, and the afternoon was spent in the performance in the open air of miracle plays, in which every craft claimed its special part. And on Midsummer Eve, these same gildsmen " - who emulated each other in the display of gay dresses, banners, burning torches, and in the supply of minstrels and musical instruments", marched through the streets, the proceedings terminating in Morris dancing and various games in which the populace participated. The mayor and his brethren of the Common Council, far from being God's ministers in punishing "dicers, mummers, ydellers, dronkerds, swearers, roges and dauncers," participated in, and even led, most of the festivities. (11)

William Canynge 1399?-1474

William Canynge was five times Mayor of Bristol and twice the Member of Parliament for the city.

Every year at Whitsuntide Saint Mary Redcliffe church is strewn with rushes and the Lord Mayor and Corporation attend service there in honour of one of Bristol's greatest citizens. The beautiful Pearl Sword is carried by the City Swordbearer. (Its scarlet scabbard is encrusted with a crown, a rose, a thistle, a harp, a dragon, three lions and the arms of Bristol, some of the motifs being wrought with seed pearls.) The sword once belonged to King Richard II, who sold it to the Corporation for £50 in order to fund his passion for feasting. (He was very imaginative in his choice of dishes, a fact that is commemorated in the nursery rhyme Four and Twenty Blackbirds Baked in a Pie.)

On an alter tomb in the south transept of St Mary Redcliffe (where Canynge is buried with his wife) is this inscription:

"Mr William, ye richest marchant of ye town of Bristow; afterwards chosen 5 times Mayor of ye said towne; for ye good of ye commonwealth of ye same: he was in order of priesthood 7 years, and afterwards Dean of Westbury, and died ye 7th of Novem. 1474, which said William did build within ye said towne of Westbury a college (with his cannons). And the said William did maintain by space of 8 years 800 handycraftsmen, besides carpenters and masons, every day 100 men."

The Early Port

At first, the quays were immediately below the walls of the castle but Bristol Bridge soon became a barrier to only the smallest ships, for there is evidence of new quays being built below the bridge at the beginning of the 13th Century, on what became known as Welsh Back and Redcliffe Back.

Until then the Frome joined the Avon just below Bristol Bridge, forming a natural moat, with an area of marsh - the Town Marsh - to the south, on the ground now occupied by Queen Square. The improvement involved cutting a trench about half a mile in length to straighten out the Frome from the bridge at St John's Gate to a new junction with the Avon downstream. The work took **eight years** to complete. The final stage involved the rebuilding of Bristol Bridge in stone, in 1247, the Avon having been diverted into a temporary channel to allow for the construction of the three massive piers that were needed to hold it up. The four-arched bridge, with houses on both sides of its 19 ft breadth was replaced in 1768 - without houses.

Going over the old bridge must have been like passing through a tunnel, for shops and houses towered above on each side, some of them five storeys high, narrowing inwards the higher they went.

Jews in old Bristol

Because they were banned from living inside the old walled town, Jews, whose only business was lending money, first settled in a confined area between St John's Gate and St Giles' Gate. Like most Jews down through the ages they suffered a lot of persecution. Once, their houses were pillaged and burned by a mob led by William Giffard, a man who had had many financial dealings with them and in **1275** decided to destroy their records and clear his debts. Another Jew who refused to pay ransom money to King John was imprisoned in Bristol castle, where torturers pulled out one of his teeth day after day. He had lost seven before he agreed to pay up!

The Discovery of America

"Of course America had often been discovered before, but it had always been hushed up." Oscar Wilde

*

John Cabot was a Venetian who became a merchant in Bristol. Here he married and had three sons, one of whom, Sebastian, he trained to become a sailor. On 5th March, **1496**, John Cabot was given authority, by Letters Patent from King Henry VII to explore easier trading routes to Asia:

"Henry, by the grace of God, King of England, France, and lord of Ireland, to all to whom these presents shall come, greeting. Be it known that we have given and granted to our well-beloved John Cabot, citizen of Venice... full and free authority, leave and power to sail to all parts, countries, and seas of the east, of the west and of the north...to seek out, discover and find ...and set up our banners and ensigns in all such newly discovered lands and subdue occupy and possess all such in the King's name."

By 2nd May **1497**, Cabot was ready to sail, in one small ship, the **Matthew**, an 80-foot, three-masted ship with a crew of eighteen. Cabot went to the west coast of Ireland, then west, "keeping the North Star on his right hand. " After fifty-three days at sea he found land, which he called "Primavista," Newfoundland.

A contemporary, writing to his family in Venice later that year said:

"The Venetian, our country-man, who went with a ship from Bristol in quest of new islands, is returned, and says that seven hundred leagues hence he discovered land, the territory of the Grand Khan. He saw no human beings, but has brought hither to the king certain snares which had been set to catch game, and a needle for making nets. He also found some felled trees, wherefore he supposed there were inhabitants, and returned to his ship in alarm. He was there three months, and on his return saw two islands, but would not land, time being precious, as he was short of provisions . . . His name is Zuan Cabot, and he is styled the great Admiral. Vast honour is paid to him; he dresses in silk, and the English run after him like mad people."

The new land was thought by Cabot to be part of the Indies. In 1497 the King granted £10 from the Privy Purse "to him that found the new isle", and a pension of **£20** annually. (Big deal.)

John Cabot *probably* died in 1498 shortly after a second voyage to North America.

A bronze tablet on St. Augustine's Bridge bears the inscription :-

From this Port
John Cabot and his son Sebastian
(who was born in Bristol)
Sailed in the ship Matthew, A.D. 1497
and
Discovered the Continent of America

In 1509 **Sebastian Cabot** set sail to see if he could discover a North-West passage across the top of Canada to the Far East. He went first to Cape Farewell, in Greenland, but was unable to go further north because the way was blocked by icebergs, so he turned west and passed through Hudson Strait to Hudson's Bay, which he took to be the Pacific Ocean. He returned to find that Henry VII had died during his absence and that the new monarch, Henry VIII, was unwilling to provide financial support for any similar ventures. He went to Spain in 1518, became Pilot-Major to the king and later sailed as leader of an expedition to South America. In 1540 he returned to Bristol.

In 1556 the "goode olde gentleman", as he had become known to some, was on board the *Seathrift*, prior to its departure on another expedition, distributing alms to the poor and asking them to pray for "good fortune and prosperous successe." The date and place of his death, and burial, are unknown.

As to his nationality, a friend recorded that "Sebastian Cabot told me that he was borne in Brystowe, and that at one yeare ould he was carried with his father to Venice, and so returned agayne into England with his father after certayne years, whereby he was thought to have been born in Venice."

However, a recent book by an American alleges that since no journal by Cabot, nor a single document in his handwriting, or even a genuine contemporary portrait exists, great doubt must attend any claim regarding his discoveries.[12]

A footnote: The Collector of Customs of the Port of Bristol was at that time a Welshman by the name of Richard ap Meryk, or Ameryk, and it is possible that the newly discovered land was later named America in his honour, and not after Amerigo Vespucci, an Italian, as is generally believed.

Imagine that! A Welshman!

The Society of Merchant Venturers

...attained independent corporate existence in **1552** when Edward VI granted a Royal Charter to "The Master, Wardens and Commonalty of Merchant Venturers of the City of Bristol." [Although there existed a hundred years before groups of merchants who could be said to be the forerunners of Edward VI's chartered Society.]

Elizabeth I, Charles I and Charles II confirmed the Society's powers by the granting of fresh Charters. In 1569 a Grant of Arms was obtained. The present constitution was set forth in the Charter granted by Charles I, by which the Master and two Wardens were given "ten of the gravest and discretest" men as Assistants. This court of 13 members still forms the executive body and is elected annually on the 10th November, the date laid down in the Charter.

In an age when exploration was taking hold upon the nation's imagination, its members played a leading part in the discovery of new lands. An ambitious venture was the equipping of an expedition in 1631 under Captain James in the Henrietta Maria of 70 tons in the hope of discovering the North-West Passage.

The early development of Newfoundland was another Society venture. John Guy, the first Governor of the Colony in 1610, was Master of the Society in 1622. During the eighteenth century Africa became an increasing source of profitable trade, and the Society fought a long and successful battle with the merchants of London, who were striving to establish a monopoly there. In 1708 the Bristol African fleet numbered nearly 60 vessels. By 1750, when a new African Company was formed, 237 of its freemen were registered in Bristol as compared with 147 in London and 89 in Liverpool.

During the war of 1756 against France, members of the Society fitted out sixty privateers, some carrying up to 36 guns, and many prizes were gained. The Admiralty placed ships of war in the port of Bristol to convoy the local West India fleets on their outward and homeward voyages and gave the Society authority to instruct the naval commanders as to date, direction and duration of each cruise. Trade increased with the Levant, the West Indies and the African colonies.

In 1779 the Society received a bequest of £1,000 from William Vick with the direction to accumulate the interest until the sum reached £10,000 and then to throw a bridge over the Avon Gorge at St. Vincent's Rocks. A Bridge Bill received the Royal Assent in May 1830 and Vick's fund, then £8,700, was handed to Trustees; this sum with other donations, including a loan and gift from the Society, amounted to £32,000. After a melancholy thirty years of costs exceeding estimates, the Suspension Bridge, to the design of Brunel, was opened in 1864.

In 1676 the Society had acquired the Manor of Clifton, then open country, which included 220 acres of Clifton Down. In 1859 the Society agreed with the Corporation of Bristol that if the Corporation would buy the Manor of Henbury, which included Durdham Down, recently placed on the market, the Society would join with the Corporation in dedicating 440 acres for the use and enjoyment of the citizens in perpetuity.

In 1921, following the example of Edward Colston, Henry Herbert Wills appointed the Society as Trustee of the St. Monica Home of Rest, built and endowed by him for chronic and incurable sufferers. St. Monica's is among the largest endowments of its kind in the United Kingdom.

For many years the Merchant Venturers had their home in Merchants' Hall in Marsh Street, a handsome building erected in the 17th Century and enlarged in 1701. This hall suffered irreparable damage in two enemy raids in December 1940 and March 1941, although fortunately the archives, plate and furnishings had been removed to places of safety. The business of the Society was carried on at the St. Monica Home of Rest until 1945, when a house was purchased at Clifton Down. The adjoining house was subsequently acquired, and in 1953 the Society adapted both houses as the new Merchants' Hall and installed the contents of the old Hall.

The Society's roll of Honorary Members shows the names of many members of the Royal House. Names famous in the country's history include amongst statesmen the Earl of Chatham, Edmund Burke, Lord North, William Pitt the Younger, George Canning, and, from the Armed Forces of the Crown, Admirals Anson, Collingwood, Rodney, Hood, and Beatty, and Field-Marshals Wellington, Roberts and Haig.

Published by the Society.

Bristol Grammar School

...was founded by Robert and Nicholas Thorne in **1532**. Its first home was St Bartholomew's Hospital, at the bottom of Christmas Steps; in 1767 it moved to Unity Street and in 1879 to the present site in Tyndall's Park.

Just over fifty years ago it survived a major physical threat which obliterated many of its neighbours. A plaque in the present Third Year block, opened in 1928 as the Preparatory School, testifies that "This building, damaged by enemy action in November and December 1940, was rebuilt in 1951 -1952".

The Bristol Police Occurrences Book'[a] gives a more dramatic minute-by-minute account of the raid on 24th November 1940:

"20.12 hrs. Grammar School burning furiously. 20.57 hrs. Fire reported at Bristol Grammar School, Light appliance has responded. 21.30 hrs. Large appliance despatched to Grammar School."

The Prep School, temporarily accommodated at Western College, Cotham Hill, and using furniture "kindly loaned to us in our dire need" by Clifton College, found a permanent home in the School House, and the school carried on. However, some concessions were made: "As a result of untimely visits by the German Air Force, morning prayers are no longer held in the Great Hall, and to avoid the foregathering of large numbers, prayers are now to be held by form masters in their own form rooms". The boys raised money for Bren Guns, trained in readiness for service in the forces, and spent hours as fire watchers. Fifty years ago the Headmaster at the Service for thanksgiving for victory in Europe recalled "the boy on fire-watching duty at the School, who, after being treated by him for a head-wound caused by our own shrapnel, said 'Won't this be something to tell my children?'"[b]

Anne Bradley, Bristol, 1995
(a) Bristol Record Office (b) BGS Chronicles 1940-45

Around 1000 ex-Grammar School boys served in the First World War. Between them they won 2 VCs, 5 DSOs, 33 MCs, 3 DCMs, and 9 Croix de Guerre. 105 of them died.

Apprentices

Indentures were enrolled at the Tolzey, "the place of common audience", which was on the corner of Corn Street and Broad Street. The Town Clerk was responsible and received 8d. "for a pair of indentures of apprentice". The mayor, sheriffs and aldermen, as justices of the peace, heard all disputes concerning contracts. The usual term of apprenticeship was seven years.

SOME INDENTURES MADE IN THE CITY OF BRISTOL IN THE YEAR OF 3 EDWARD VI [1549]

September 30: **John** s of Richard **Kennyk**, Taunton Somerset, saddler to John Michell **saddler** and Christiana wf for 7 yrs, to have at end 20/- etc.

November 12: **Katharine** d of William **Denis** late Bristol, shearman dec to William Jaie **merchant** and Alice wf for 10 yrs etc.

November 14: **Alice** d of Thomas **Lunedon**, Linkeloll [Linkenholt] Hants, husbandman to Lionel Colman **fishmonger** and Elizabeth wf for 7 yrs etc.

November 16: **Alexander** s of Bartholomew **Newton**, Bodnam [Bodenham] Hereford East, **husbandman to** David Harte shearman and Margaret wf for 7 yrs to have at end 20/-.

During the period 1542-1552, about 1800 apprentices were enrolled, of which 50 were women. Of the 50 women, seven were apprenticed as seamstresses, seventeen as housewives. In several cases the master had to send the boy to school for a year or more, and in two cases "until he can profitely write and rede" or "write and read and caste accompt". Young men apprenticed to merchants were often sent overseas to gain experience, usually to Spain and Portugal, but sometimes to Flanders and France, at the expense of their masters.[14]

Bigotry

In those days most people went to church on a Sunday, but times were brutal. In **1555** five working class men were burnt to death on St. Michael's Hill, on the site of Highbury Chapel, for maintaining the Protestant faith despite Queen Mary's attempts to restore Roman Catholicism.

A tablet is erected to their memory in the chapel, the inscription of which reads:

"In Memory of the undernamed Martyrs, who, during the reign of Queen Mary, for the avowal of their Christian faith, were burnt to death on the ground upon which this Chapel is erected.

"William Shapton, suffered October 17th, 1555.
Edward Sharp, September 8th, 1556.
Richard Sharp, May 17th, 1557.
Thomas Hale, May 17th, 1557.
Thomas Banion, August 17th, 1557.

"Be not afraid of them that kill the body and after that have no more that they can do."

In 1558 Elizabeth I became queen. It was during her reign that the first map of Bristol was made, by a man called William Smith, in1568 after a two day visit! It was published in Cologne in a book that purported to portray some of the most important towns in the then known world. At the time there were only 6,000 inhabitants in the city, and they all lived within the same small walled area that had already existed for centuries. People did not like to live outside the safety of the walls, and it would be some time before the expanding population obliged them to do so.

ROYAL VISITS

Queen Elizabeth I visited Bristol in **1574**. Since such honour accrued from rare opportunities to entertain royalty, every effort was made to show the City at its best. During the visit "the mayor and all the council riding upon good steeds, with footcloths, and pages by their sides" received Her Majesty within Lawford's Gate, just outside the boundaries of the city. "At the gate the mayor delivered [his] mace unto her Grace," thus relinquishing the sign of his authority as her lieutenant, "and she delivered it unto him again," reinforcing her authority over the city and his dependence upon her for favour. After an oration by John Popham, the recorder, and the presentation of a gift of **£100** in gold to her, the queen was escorted through the city in a procession in which "the mayor himself rode nigh before the Queene, betweene 2 serjeants at arms." This procession, with each rider holding his proper place in relation to the queen and the others in the order of march, set the tone for the military displays that occupied the queen's time for the rest of her three-day stay. (11)

Queen Victoria knighting Herbert Ashman after he was created the first Lord Mayor of Bristol in 1899.

Queen Elizabeth's Hospital School

The first school to be established in the buildings of the dissolved Hospital of the Gaunts was Queen Elizabeth's Hospital, which was founded by John Carr, a soap merchant, in **1590**, on the model of Christ's Hospital, London. A royal charter was granted by Queen Elizabeth I in the same year.

Bristolians who watch the boys of Queen Elizabeth's Hospital school file into the Lord Mayor's Chapel for Council Prayers wearing their traditional dress are seeing living history. The blue-coats, girdles, preaching bands, moleskin breeches and bright yellow socks of pupils at what is sometimes called "The City School" have survived four centuries of change.

Stories are still told concerning the ghost of a matron called the Grey Lady, who is supposed to have thrown herself off the battlements after her fiancee was killed in the Great War. Another ghost is that of a boy who fell from The Upper and died in the yard (supposedly the largest paved area in the city). The present buildings were constructed over a Jewish graveyard, but its residents seem to sleep in peace.

Even in the 18th Century, Bristolians must have gossiped about political "sleaze". The Corporation, as trustees, had built a light, airy and healthy new school for the QEH boys in Orchard Street. The only daughter of an influential alderman married the headmaster of the Grammar School, at that time housed in dilapidated and unhealthy quarters at the bottom of Christmas Steps. The Corporation persuaded the two schools to change quarters and the alderman's daughter was soon living in the new building, away from the "smelly and unwholesome" River Frome.

In time it was discovered that since 1590 the School's Foundation income had been subverted by the Corporation - they had met the running costs and kept the profits rather than reinvesting them for the school's benefit. Major scandal was avoided by an out-of-court settlement which left QEH as the best endowed school in the city, but still poorer by many millions of pounds (in today's terms) than it should have been.

Susan Bladon, Bristol, 1995

Ale Tasters

In the 17th Century Bristol Corporation had two ale tasters on its payroll. They were paid 53s.4d. **per year,** reduced to 40s in 1622. Their duties were to taste the ale brewed for Bristolians and to inform against "knavish brewers." What a job, for which there must have been hundreds of applicants. In those days beer cost 2₁/₂d, a gallon! It is probable that they seldom, if ever, needed to call at...

The Wine Street Pump

which was sunk somewhere about the year **1625**. It was then, probably, a wooden one, but never since has it refused to fill the kettles of the citizens of Wine Street; and no doubt helped to brew as many bowls of punch as dishes of tea.

Wine Street Pump was standing, and probably helped to support some spectators, on 30th May 1643, when Mr. Yeamans and Mr. Boucher, both citizens of high honour and station, were hanged close by for the "crime" of "endeavouring to restore Bristol to its rightful sovereign, from the hands of a parcel of prick-eared Republicans". As those two noble men were being turned off, many were struck down for praying for them. One can imagine Wine Street at that moment, the windows full of spectators, the pavements packed with a great crowd, above whose heads two of its chief citizens stood on a scaffold, with Master Baugh - the sheepskin-dresser volunteer hangman for the occasion - by their side. (15)

In Medieval times Wine Street was one of the four - High, Broad and Corn - streets that were at the very heart of the city. They were busy shopping centres, filled with crowds of people. In 1698 Celia Fiennes described the scene: "The buildings of the town are pretty high, most of timber work, the streets narrow and something darkish because the roomes on the upper stories jut out." One of them was the 17th Century battlemented Dutch House, its rows of windows looking like the stern post of a man-o-war and adorned with a carving of a wooden soldier. Sadly, much of that old Bristol, which would have been a delight to walk in today, was destroyed in the Blitz.

Artist's impression of Ye Olde Llandoger Trow building when it was a merchant's property and before it became a pub and was called that.

The old Dutch House, a medieval building destroyed in the blitz.

The Nails in Corn Street, the origin of the phrase "Paying on the Nail", when merchants struck their bargains and sealed them "on the nail."

HMS Bristol, around the year 1800, and under it a view of Bristol port as she might have known it, a picture painted by W.J.Muller in 1837.

The man and one of his many monuments. Isambard Kingdom Brunel
and the suspension bridge during its construction.

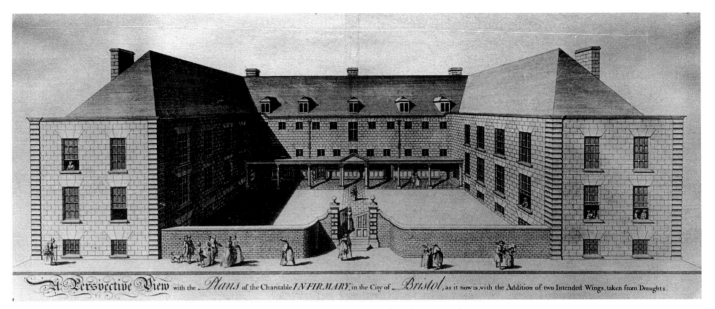

Plan of the Bristol Royal Infirmary drawn up in 1743 and a photograph taken during the opening of the new buildings in 1929. Today, the infirmary pioneers new techniques as well as, together with the other great Bristol hospitals, caring for our citizens.

Red Maids Angela Freeman and Eva Wong in St Nicholas church crypt, November 1981

The Red Maids' School

is the oldest surviving girls' school in the country. It was founded in **1634** as the result of the benevolence of John Whitson, merchant, Mayor of Bristol and Member of Parliament.

Of his time in London, Whitson declared 'I daily learnt new lessons of the world's vanity, and augmented my grief together with my experience,' but depressed by the world or not, he was forward-thinking enough to endow a school for girls, perhaps because he himself had three daughters, and survived them all. How his widow - his third wife - felt when he left much of his property to charitable purposes is indicated by her challenge to his Will, which delayed the school's establishment until five years after his death.

The school owes its name to John Whitson's expressed wish that the 'poor women' for whom he was providing should 'go and be apparelled in red cloth.' The uniform is never more apparent than in November, when the school honours its founder in a ceremony which is the highlight of the city calendar. The whole school processes through the streets of Bristol from Whitson's tomb in St Nicholas' church to a service of thanksgiving in the cathedral. Boarders are clad in traditional uniform of scarlet cloaks and straw bonnets, and the traffic of the city is stopped for the occasion by a mounted police escort. Early this century the Red Maids School moved from its original city home to spacious accommodation in Westbury-on-Trym, where it flourishes today.

Hilary Moriarty, Monmouth, 1995

Occupations of Bristol Aldermen, 1605 - 1642

Merchants 19, Apothecary 1, Grocer 1, Drapers 3, Hardwareman 1, Mercers 6, Vintner 1, Soapmakers, Chandlers 2, Clothiers 2, Cardmaker 1, Brewers 2, Yeomen 3.

(Total, 42)

The Civil War

The importance of Bristol to the Royalist cause was that the town, of some 15,000 to 20,000, inhabitants held a dominating position in the west. At the opening of the war the King's influence was strongest in the north and west; that of Parliament in the south and east. With Gloucester and Bristol both in Parliamentary hands, the junction of the King's supporters in the north and Wales with those from Cornwall was a very difficult matter, and the capture of both towns was looked upon as a necessary preliminary to any advance upon London, which, of course, was the key to the whole situation.[1]

The neutral stance adopted by the Councillors of Bristol at the start of the war quickly became untenable; the city's strategic and economic importance to both sides was far too great for it to remain unmolested for long. After several months of prevarication by the city authorities, Bristol was occupied on 9 December **1642** by Parliamentarian troops under Colonel Thomas Essex; they seem to have met little or no resistance. On 27 February 1643 Essex, whose increasingly erratic behaviour had aroused the suspicions of his superiors, was arrested and replaced as governor by Colonel Nathaniel Fiennes, son of the leading Parliamentarian Lord Saye and Sele. On 8 March Fiennes uncovered and crushed a major plot by Royalist sympathisers to open the city to Prince Rupert, whose troops had been observed massing to the north of the town; two of the ringleaders, Robert Yeamans and George Bowcher, were executed in Wine Street on 30 May.

On 5-6th July 1643 Bristolians were able to witness from a distance a bloody but indecisive encounter between the main Parliamentarian army in the Southwest, commanded by Sir William Waller, and the Royalist "Western Army" under Sir Ralph Hopton, the Marquess of Hertford, and Prince Maurice, on the Lansdown ridge to the north of Bath. A week later Waller's forces were effectively destroyed by the loyalists at Roundway Down near Devizes. Waller retreated, leaving Fiennes with a seriously depleted garrison. Seeking to exploit this weakness a Royalist army under Prince Rupert marched south from Oxford on 18th July, reaching Westbury-on-Trym five days later. On 24-25 July Rupert deployed his forces around the northern edge of the city, facing the defensive line newly constructed by the Parliamentarians. [23]

Rupert had 20,000 men, the Governor of Bristol, Colonel Fiennes, had only 2,300. Nevertheless, the town's defences seemed strong, and Rupert was lacking in cannon. He remedied this by the capture of eight ships in the Kingroad (off Avonmouth), the guns of which were quickly brought ashore.

Little headway was made on the Monday and the attacks throughout Tuesday were without result, so it was decided to make a general assault upon the defences at six different points. At Temple Gate and Redcliffe Gate, Stokes Croft and St. Michael's Hill, the besiegers were repulsed. At Prior's Hill Fort, in spite of the weak state of the rampart, Blake (who later became famous as an admiral) held off the attack, and it seemed as if Rupert was doomed to failure; but success came to him from an unexpected quarter. The story is best told in the words of Mistress Dorothy Hazard, wife of the minister of St. Ewen's Church, and a prominent Puritan.

"I was in the city during the siege when Colonel Nathaniel Fiennes was governor there. When the news came on the Wednesday morning that some of the enemy were entered within the line, with divers other women and maydes, with the help of some men, I did, with wool-sacks and earth, stop up Froome Gate to keep out the enemy from entering the city, being the only passage by which the enemy must enter, and when they had so done the women went to the gunners and told them that if they would stand and fight we would stand by them, but the Governor had treated with the enemy and yielded up the city and castle to them."[1]

On 25th July the Royalist leaders met at Knowle and determined (not without some dispute) to attempt to take the city by storm rather than by a prolonged siege. Their attack began in the early hours of the following day, Wednesday 26th July. Initial assaults by the northern "Oxford Army" on Stokes Croft Gate, Priors Hill Fort and the defences to the north-east of Windmill Hill Fort proved costly and ineffective, while attempts by the Western Army to take the southern Port Wall were similarly repulsed with heavy losses.

43

Eventually, however, troops led by Colonel Henry Washington broke through the northern defences in the valley between Brandon Hill and Windmill Hill Forts. After further fierce fighting in the north-western suburbs and around the Frome Gate (during which the Royalists sustained further heavy casualties) Fiennes sought terms for surrender.[24] This was probably the only realistic option, since Fiennes' troops numbered no more than 2,500 against a besieging force of at least 14,000. His capitulation nevertheless attracted savage criticism, particularly from local Parliamentarians whose property had been looted by the victorious Royalists.

In December 1643 Fiennes was brought to trial at St Albans for his alleged cowardice and treachery and condemned to death, although he was subsequently pardoned through his father's intervention. The capture of a major port and regional centre such as Bristol represented a much-needed success for the Royalists, albeit a costly one; their casualties were numerous, including many brave and experienced officers. On 3rd August 1643 Charles I visited the city and installed Rupert as governor, with Sir Ralph (now Lord) Hopton as his deputy.[23]

Once in the city the Royalists got out of control. Many of the defenders were robbed of all they possessed and many houses were sacked. Tradesmen were robbed of their goods and, to crown all, Royalists were billeted on the inhabitants, twenty or thirty to a house in some instances, the citizens being turned out of their beds to make room.[1]

No further significant fighting took place, in the Bristol area until the summer of 1645, the Parliamentarian assault finally beginning before dawn on 10th September. It was concentrated on the eastern sector of the defences. The defenders of Priors Hill held out obstinately for several hours, being eventually massacred for their intransigence. Elsewhere, however, the defences were breached with relative ease and the Parliamentarians were able to advance towards the heart of the city. At this point Rupert seems to have judged that further resistance was pointless, and offered to surrender; on the following day he led his defeated forces out of the city. The inability of the charismatic Royalist leader to hold Bristol provoked a furious reaction from the King, while at the same time prompting many Parliamentarians to take a more sympathetic view of Fiennes' behaviour two years previously.

There was an aftermath...

In **1655** Oliver Cromwell ordered that the mighty Bristol castle should be demolished. Work began on 4th January, 1656 but by October so little had been done that the magistrates ordered each citizen to pay a labourer's wages one day in each week until the task was finished. This brought such a speedy response that within two weeks a building that had dwarfed the city churches for centuries had vanished!

Almost nothing remains of this great castle, which had seven towers and a great keep and was exceeded in size only by Colchester and the Tower of London, except that in Tower Street there are two 13th Century vaulted chambers which probably formed the entrance to the banqueting hall. (6)

One of the reasons why Bristol was of great importance to Cromwell during the Civil war was that he regarded it as "an ever-open door to the dreaded possibility of Irish or even continental assistance for the King," Bristol having traded with Ireland for centuries and there therefore being a host of contacts between Royalist Bristolians and their Irish friends. When after the siege he came to Bristol (when a public holiday was declared) he told his soldiers that "they were Israelites about to extirpate the idolatrous inhabitants of Canaan". It seems doubtful that they recognised themselves in that description, even if they understood what he was talking about.

Samuel Pepys visited Bristol

...on 13th June **1668** with his wife and her pretty maid, Deb Willet. The coach which brought the party from Bath set them down at the "Horse Shoe", a posting house, where Pepys was "trimmed" by a barber for ten shillings. (Which seems an awful lot of money, for those days.) Pepys diary records:-

"Walked with my wife and people through the city, which is in every respect another London that one can hardly know it stands in the country. **No carts, it standing generally on vaults, only dog-carts."** Deb went to see her Uncle Butts, so Pepys, leaving his wife at the "Sun" set off... "to see the Key, which is a large and noble place; and to see the new ship a'building. It will be a fine ship, and walked back to the Sun, where I find Deb come back, and with her, her uncle, a sober merchant, very good company, and so like one of our sober wealthy London merchants, as pleased me mightily. Where we dined, and much good talk with me. Then walked with Butts and my wife and company round the Key, and he showed me the Custom House, and made me understand many things of the place, and led me through Marsh Street where our girl (Deb) was born. But Lord! the joy that was among the old people of the place, to see Mrs. Willet's daughter, it seems her mother being a brave woman and mightily beloved! And brought us back by surprise to his house, where a substantial good house, and well furnished; and did give us good entertainment of strawberries, a whole venison pasty, and plenty of brave wine, and above all Bristol Milk: where comes in another poor woman, who, hearing that Deb was here, did come running hither, and with her eyes so full of tears, and her heart so full of joy, that she could not speak when she came in, that it made me weep too. So thence took leave, and he with us through the city. He showed us the place where the merchants meet here, and a fine cross yet standing like Cheapside. And so to the Horse Shoe and by moonshine to Bath again, about ten o'clock."

And Confirmation...

"A few churches of eminent beauty rose out of a labyrinth of narrow lanes built upon vaults of no great solidity. If a coach or a cart entered these alleys, there was danger that it would be wedged between the houses, and danger also that it would break into the cellars. *Goods were therefore conveyed about the town almost exclusively in trucks drawn by dogs;* and the richest inhabitants exhibited their wealth, not by riding in gilded carriages, but by walking the streets with trains of servants in rich liveries, and by keeping tables loaded with good cheer. *The pomp of the christenings and burials far exceeded what was seen at any other place in England.* The hospitality of the city was widely renowned, and especially the collations with which the sugar refiners regaled their visitors. The repast was accompanied by a rich brewage made of the best Spanish wine, *and celebrated over the whole kingdom as Bristol Milk.*"

(Macaulay's History of England, 1855.)

And here are some quotes from Pepys

"Strange to say what delight we married people have to see these poor fools decoyed into our condition."

a touch of spleen, mirroring -

"I find that my wife has something in her gizzard that only wants an opportunity of being provoked to bring it up!"

perhaps because..

"My wife, poor wretch, is troubled with her lonely life."

due to too many evenings on her own while he enjoyed other pleasures!

47

Old Bristol

In the 14th Century the population, based on the **Poll Tax** returns of 1377, was between 9,500 and 12,000. There is no means of saying how many of these people were engaged in industry, how many in providing services of various kinds and how many in overseas trade, but foreign commerce, particularly in cloth, wine and **woad(!)**, was of major importance. Between September 1479 and July 1480, for example, some 150 individuals are recorded as trading with Gascony, Spain and Portugal alone. Many of the people were not, of course, full-time merchants, for there seems have been nothing to stop anybody who wished to do so from engaging in an occasional venture overseas, but there is plenty of evidence to show that there was a group of wealthy men whose main business was import and export. These professional merchants played a predominant part in governing the city, and they used some of their wealth for the enrichment of the churches and for charitable activities of many kinds. (And still do, as members of the Society of Merchant Venturers.)

In Henry VIII's reign the population of Bristol had stood at about ten thousand persons, not far different from what it had probably been in the aftermath of the Black Death in the 14th century. Late in Elizabeth I's reign it began to grow, and by the beginning of James I's reign it had reached twelve thousand, or perhaps a bit higher. In the early 1670s it seems to have been about sixteen thousand, and at the end of the 17th Century it had exceeded twenty thousand. The next century witnessed a doubling in size, as Bristol's built-up area burst beyond the boundaries of the small medieval city [in which there were seventeen parishes and twenty churches] and spread into the surrounding countryside.

This sets the 17th Century apart as the beginning of a new period in Bristol's long-term development. No longer was its population essentially stable in size, with every increase in the number of inhabitants almost immediately cut back by epidemic disease, as had happened periodically from the late 14th to the late 16th century. Even the great plague that killed between 2,500 and 3,000 Bristolians in 1603 and 1604 was unable to stop the steady growth of the City. Within five years the population had already made up between 50 and 75 percent of the loss.

A second great plague in 1645, which killed three thousand inhabitants in the course of the New Model Army's siege of the city * in that year, also resulted in a rapid recovery. By 1600 Bristol had become a city of ever-expanding numbers, growing in size slowly at first but with increasing momentum. In 1700 it was twice as large as it had been in 1550.(11)

* [Most of the victims were buried on Broadmead, on land that is under what is now Lewis' store!]

As the 19th Century entered its third decade, Bristol continued to expand, both in physical extent and in population. Medieval Bristol, the seventeen original parishes centering on the fork between the river Frome and the old course of the Avon, was...a shrinking nucleus of the built-up area. Recent growth had transformed St. Michael, St. James, St. Paul and St Augustine into populous parishes, yet they were being over-shadowed by Clifton's development as a fashionable suburb and Bedminster's new role as an area into which the working class was migrating. (16)

By the last year of the 17th Century Bristol contained just under three thousand five hundred houses, with a population of about thirty thousand, thus tying with Norwich for second place to London. In the following year the Marsh was drained and Queen's Square was cut.(5) The central city, infested with dank, dark lanes, was no longer capable of containing the thrust of commercial demands and the grander aspirations of many inhabitants. In two decades Bristol's population rose by over 20,000. By 1821, Bristol was on the verge of containing 100,000 people. Ten years later, the figure was 117,016. (16)

The streets had been constructed for a far less congested life. Their average width was less than twenty feet, while the houses, chiefly of timber and plaster, overhung the roads. There were no pavements and the roads themselves were roughly paved with stone blocks, with a channel down the centre. Pigs nosed among the garbage in this open drain, and in spite of the fact that at one time an official was employed to cut off the tails of the offending animals, the nuisance continued. Sanitation received scant consideration. There were no underground sewers, the Avon and Frome doing service instead. The water supply was far from satisfactory. It is not surprising that visitations the plague were fairly frequent. (11)

49

Food was lacking in variety, for until the introduction of root crops for cattle food about 1730, there was little fresh meat to be had in winter, and until the breeding of cattle was improved they were, by modern standards, scraggy and bony. Canning and refrigeration had not yet solved the problem of the [preservation and] import of perishable goods. Even so, the gentry in Bristol managed to load their tables well. They drank deeply, too, of port, spirits, beer, cider and perry. Tea and coffee were popular. The majority of people had three meals a day, at about 7 a.m., noon and 6 p.m., though among the upper classes dinner was usually about 2 p.m.

Though the few wealthy people ate well, the many ate meat once a week if they were lucky, and subsisted on bread, pulses and cheap ale - the water was deadly. Generally, the labouring classes fared badly. In Bristol the wages of labourers in different factories varied from 7/- to 35/- per week, though the average seems to have been in the neighbourhood of 10/- to 15/-. Common Labourers earned 1/6 per day, "without victuals". Children employed in cotton manufacture earned 1/6 to 3/- per week. Against this, the common prices of necessities were:

Beef, 4½d, to 5d. per lb.	Mutton, 5d. to 6d. per lb.
Veal, 6d. per lb.	Bacon, 9d. to 10d. per lb.
Butter, 11d. to 1/- per lb.	Potatoes, 6d. per peck.
Bread, 1/- for 4-lb. loaf.	Coals, 3½d. a bushel.

As an example, [at the beginning of the 18th Century] a Bristol labourer, 50 years of age, with a wife and two children, one five years old and the other nine months worked at an inn, as a horse keeper, porter etc., and earned the sum of 9/- per week. His wife earned an occasional shilling by washing.

The weekly family expenditure included bread 4/6, meat 6d., butter (1/2-lb.) 5½d., cheese (1/2-lb.) 3d., tea 3d., potatoes (2 pecks) 1/-, milk (1/2-pint a day for the child) 3d., candles, soap etc 5d. No allowance was made for clothing, obtained usually through charity. When darkness fell it was time for bed, since only the rich could afford good candles.(1)

More Bigotry, in the 17th Century

The City Council was largely in favour of the Dissenters [Protestant non-conformists], and went so far as to elect as Mayor, in **1670**, a man named John Knight who was well known as a sympathiser. The Government ordered a re-election but the Council boldly refused to give way. The new Mayor was called to London, but when he was faced with his accuser before the King, the latter "having regard to the good character he had received of him," allowed him to depart. He was received back in Bristol by no less than 235 horsemen, amid the rejoicings of the townsfolk. But the good days did not last. Bishop Ironside was succeeded by Bishop Carleton, a violent persecutor. Then, in 1674 Ralph Ollive was elected as mayor. He was the landlord of the Three Tuns Tavern, and a hater of dissenters. Two sheriffs of similar opinions were appointed and persecution then began in earnest.

The Dissenters had recently been worshipping without interference under special licences from the King. Bishop Carleton went to London and secured the cancellation of these licences. "His tribe speedily then began very vigorously to bestir themselves, and lost no time; for the very same week the bishop, with divers of his clergy, got some of the aldermen and some of the military officers together, and went to Mr. Thompson's meeting, in the Castle where, finding him preaching they, after search, met with him, and brought him before the Mayor to his mansion house, where, after long examination and discourse about nine of the clock at night, the Mayor, bishop and some aldermen commit Mr. Thompson to Newgate prison [in Bristol] for six months."

The minister was very sick when he went to jail "and although divers persons of note in this city, in the compassion of their hearts for this sick minister, did go to the mayor and sheriffs, and to Sir John Knight, to get leave that he might be permitted to go home, they could not prevail. And his physician interceded that he might be removed out of that stinking prison, to some convenient house for air, and to minister more conveniently to him, and he showed the danger of his condition; yet, notwithstanding, they hardened their hearts, and would not grant it because the bishop would not give leave." The unfortunate Thompson died on March 4th. **Five thousand** people attended his funeral at St. Philip's church, and threats of rebellion were heard.

At last the landlord mayor's term of office came to an end and for a time the persecution ceased, but in 1681 it broke out with renewed vigour. In November of that year all the non-conformist ministers of the town, and about a hundred laymen, were cast into prison. First the Presbyterian Chapel and then the Quakers' Friars and the Broadmead chapel were broken into and wrecked. Within a few weeks the other Chapels were wrecked - windows broken, doors nailed up and ministers sent to jail. Even boys, who could not be punished under the Acts, were put in the stocks and beaten with whalebone rods for holding prayer meetings whilst their parents were in jail, while fifteen boys and girls were put into the Bridewell "for disturbing the peace". Once again meetings were held in the fields outside the town, but even here they were attacked by bands of ruffians employed by the magistrates. Newgate was so full that the prisoners had to sleep four on a pallet. The Quakers bore the brunt of the attacks, and in the year 1683 alone fines amounting to £16,440 were imposed upon them. [1]

Judge Jeffreys

In **1685** the mayor of Bristol received a sharp rebuke from Jeffreys when he came to try the accused men of the Monmouth Rebellion. Having condemned six rebels to death (three were later reprieved, three were hung on Redcliffe Hill) he rounded on the mayor as "a knave and a kidnapper" and ordered him to stand in the dock, then fined him £1,000 "for suffering a boy committed to Bridewell to go beyond the Sea": the mayor had followed the custom of reprieving criminals sentenced to death on condition they agreed to work on plantations in the West Indies.

Jeffreys was only 37 when he was made a judge. He was often in pain, drank heavily to dull it and would listen to no defence during trials. In all, 233 persons were hanged, drawn, quartered and gibbeted at cross-roads, market places and village greens in the West country. Another 850 were transported to the West Indies. What an epitaph!

Big Bristol

In **1699,** when Parliament voted a grant to the Navy, only Norwich and London were Assessed at a higher rate than Bristol. In 1701 there were 165 ships, of an average of 105 tons, sailing from Bristol; Newcastle came next on the list with 163 ships, averaging 73 tons. By the beginning of the 18th Century Bristol had become the third richest town in the kingdom, and the greatest port outside London.[7]

"In the middle of the streets, as far as you can see, are hundreds of ships, their masts as thick as they can stand by one another, which is the oddest and most surprising sight imaginable."

Alexander Pope, in 1732

A Great Storm

"This day, the XVth of October **1747**, was the grettest flode and the grettist wynde at Bristowe and in the cuntrey there abouts that ever was seen, and grete hurt doon in the merchaunts' sellers in wode (woad) and salt; a shippe lost at Kyngrode, the Anthony of Bristowe, and a ship of Bilbowe set a-land at Holow bakkes, and other botes lost; saltmarsh drowned, corne, catell, and houses borne away with the sea, and moche people drowned, to the nommebre of C.C. [200] and more."

A contemporary account. See by comparison the report by Terry Staples of the flood of 1968 on pages 147 and 148. When will the next one be, I wonder?

SLAVERY

As the premier slave-trading city in Europe in the 18th Century, Liverpool has not unnaturally attracted most of the attention of students of the British slave trade.   The fact is, however, that Bristol was a greater slaving port than Liverpool for most of the first half of the 18th Century, and continued to be involved seriously up to and even beyond the War of American Independence. Furthermore, Bristol's participation in slaving over the course of the whole 18th Century was significantly greater than any of the major French ports whose slaving activities have been so meticulously documented recently.(17)

A prominent feature in the history of Bristol in the 18th Century is one that is by no means to the credit of the city. Horrible details are on record of the brutalities of the Bristol slave trade, but yet so tenacious and so influential were the dealers in human beings that **the bells of the city churches were rung merrily** upon the rejection of Wilberforce's anti-slavery Bill. (5)

In a voyage in 1729 aboard a ship called "John and Betty", the slaves were reported to have been "the worst Cargoe of Negroes to have been imported for several Years past". Eleven or more were said to have died since their arrival and planters would not buy the cargo when it was offered for sale on 10 November. l05 were sold to Lamego & Furtado at £18.10s.0d. each; the factors, Tyndall & Assheton, thought the remainder so bad they could not get £8 per head for them and would have to auction them "for the most they will Yield".

In the same year, aboard a ship called "The Cornwall", the slaves were expected to average £24 to £25 per head when sold in Jamaica. The cargo included 30 boys and girls. Half of the vessel's slaves were reported to have been shipped to South Keys, where it was said "there is a vast Demand and Good Price, Generally 125 to 130 Dollars Men & Women, and from $15 to $17 advance in the Money". (17)

Tobacco

The industry in which H. O. Wills decided to seek his fortune [in 1777] had its origins in the late 16th Century. Despite James I's famous pamphlet of 1604, *A Counterblaste to Tobacco*, which among other things claimed that smoking was a sin, and despite more practical attempts to impose a prohibitive duty on tobacco imports, the popularity of tobacco spread. According to Barnaby Rich, in *Honesty of this Age* (1614) 'tobacco is now as vendible in every tavern, inn and ale house, as either wine, ale, or beer', and it could be purchased as easily in apothecaries' shops, grocers' shops, chandlers' shops. Indeed, in the 17th Century much of the trade in selling tobacco was done by apothecaries because it was regarded as a herb of considerable prophylactic and medicinal value! Soon, however, smoking and snuff-taking came to be appreciated as pleasures in themselves, and once the fashion caught on retailers of various kinds were quite willing to add tobacco to their wares.

There were three main products: cut tobacco, roll tobacco and snuff. The varieties of leaf most used came from places closely associated with the early English settlements of North America - from York River, James River, and Carolina. The leaf was imported in hogsheads weighing approximately 1,000 lb, and if it was in a very dry condition it was necessary to moisten it before handling. The first operation was the removal of the stem and rib from the leaf to obtain 'strips', work done by women using short, sharp, knives. A particularly skilled worker could earn what was then the relatively high wage of 12s. to 15s a week. (Any tobacco left on the stalks was picked off by hand. In 1939 the wage of a tobacco stripper was ten shillings and sixpence per week.)

The next process was to fix the moisture content of the leaf, according to the flavour and type of tobacco required and in order to preserve it. To do this strips were placed in heaps to which water was added; additives such as sugar, glycerine, gum and starch were in common use. The 'liquor' caused the tobacco to ferment; the fumes produced by fermentation were sometimes so pungent that workmen could not endure them even "with the aid of open doors, windows and chimneys, and all the assistance that could be given them". (5)

And Chocolate

Chocolate drinking was certainly known in Bristol by **1700**, soon after its first coming to this country, and chocolate houses were built on Clifton Downs. Then in the 18th Century we get clear knowledge of Bristol's manufacture of chocolate; the pioneers were apothecaries, running a sideline in their ordinary business. Later we find it as the stock-in-trade of grocers or of dealers in coffee and tea.

In 1731 a man by the name of Walter Churchman was granted a patent for a machine used to make chocolate. In **1761** Churchman's son sold the patent to a Quaker apothecary by the name of Joseph Fry. In 1777 he moved the factory to Union Street.[18]

Street names.

Whiteladies Road: Nuns who wore white habits lived in a nunnery on this road.

Clare Street: Similarly, nuns of the order of the Poor Clares lived on this street.

Lady's Mile. In complete contrast, whores plied their trade (or should it be 'profession', the oldest in the world, so it is said?) along this road across the Downs. (Sometimes, they still do!)

Blackboy Hill. Slaves probably lived in shacks near this road and were hired out for labour, but generally few slaves were brought to Bristol; the money was to be had by taking them to America and the West Indies and selling them to work in the plantations.

And how about?

Zed Alley, There and Back Again Lane, Cat Brain Lane, Johnny Ball Lane, Christmas Steps, Washing Pound Lane, Pipe Lane.

They all have a special meaning, though nowadays most people have forgotten what it was.

56

18th Century Smuggling

The word "Geneva" is derived from the French 'genevre' - juniper. The spirit was first introduced into the country by William III, around 1700. Sales were slow, but soon English distillers found how cheap it was to produce, and within a short time sales of gin far exceeded that of beer. It could be purchased for as little as 9d per gallon and was sold for **4s a gallon;** and could be bought almost anywhere, even from street barrows and carts. The sign 'Drunk for 1d, Dead Drunk for 2d, Straw for nothing' appeared in the windows of shops and inns. [The straw was for lying on to sleep off the effects!] Gin became the drink of the working classes. By the end of the century it had once again achieved respectability as a 'middle-class' drink, largely as a result of smuggling.

There were various categories of men involved: landers, tubmen, look-out men and batmen, who were normally recruited on a nightly basis from the labouring poor of the port and were, more often than not, farm workers. Generally they would receive 10s for a few hours work, as well as a free dollop of tea and maybe some Geneva. [Which compared very favourably with the average weekly wage for a farm hand of 10s. A wage, incidentally, that would continue to be the norm until the beginning of the 20th Century.]

The tubmen had the most physically demanding job of all: employed as human packhorses to carry two half-ankers (about 4 gallons each) of spirit slung over their shoulders. [Thomas Hardy tells of an old tubman who remembered "the horribly suffocating sensation" induced by the burden of a pair of spirit tubs carried for several miles over rough country and in darkness.] Because Customs had the legal right to impose penalties for minor smuggling offences there are many recorded instances of tubmen spending months in jail for debt. During the French wars many of them were "pressed", either into the Navy or the Army.

As for the batmen, as their name implies they carried 'bats': stout wooden staves, often iron-tipped and at least six feet long, to enable them to ward off the swords and cutlasses of the Revenue men - which were also an effective weapon to unseat men on horseback.

The batmen were, in essence, the security guards, who were there to protect the valuable cargo and assist the nucleus of regular gang-members, who always rode well-armed with pistols, swords and loaded whips. Smugglers received almost universal support from the rest of the community; farmers willingly left stables and barns unlocked to allow the smugglers to 'borrow' their animals and carts; packages of tea and gin were left for them when their property was returned.

There is an old West Country saying that "Smuggling money never did good to anyone," and one old Cornish smuggler maintained that "One moment there would be money and to spare, but it would be lost later on; and every smuggler that I remember died poor." Perhaps he was right but he was not speaking about the smuggling kings, whose profits were enormous and whose losses - certainly as far as the Bristol Channel was concerned - were minimal. [19]

The Llandoger Trow

This famous inn was originally one of a number of timber-framed houses built near the quayside by wealthy merchants in the 17th Century. The *Trow* takes its name from the flat-bottomed sailing barges used by merchants who traded from nearby Welsh Back. The *Llandoger* part of the title is probably associated with the village of Llandogo on the Wye. It, and other inns like it, were used for the recruitment - and sometimes impressment - of sailors.

The Hole In The Wall

More a long slit
Like, and Tom,
That's where he sit
And watch out
For the Press Gang.

Tom left a hand
At the Nile, see,
So they don't want 'e,
Boy. When Tom gives
The "Look alive"
Then you nip
Down them stairs
Back of the bar.

Slow on the rum,
Cos if you slip,
Like what Joe
Did, you're Jack Tar
'Fore you knows
Where you are.

Take me, never meant
For the sea.
(T'isn't the Captain
'Tis conditions, boy,
Don't know how
I come through.)
So when you
Hear Tom shout -
It's down to the
Cellar, boy, and **OUT**.

Claire Hall(10)

Taking the Waters

The Hotwell spring was first mentioned in the 15th Century by the Bristol chronicler William of Wyrecestre. A spring gushed out of an opening at the foot of St.Vincent's rock in the Avon Gorge at the rate of 60 gallons a minute, at a temperature of 76 degrees.

In 1696 Hotwell House was built on a small rock ledge jutting out into the river after the lords of the manor of Clifton, the Society of Merchant Venturers, leased the Hot Well to a group of investors. Pumps raised the water 30ft to the new Pump Room. The waters became known in the later 17th Century as a cure for kidney troubles and diabetes, and towards the end of the 18th century were used to treat tuberculosis.

Between **1760** and **1790** Hotwell House was *the* place to go if you wanted to mingle with the famous. But there were snags; reaching the spa involved negotiating a rough track and descending 200 slippery steps. Despite that, among those who came to take the waters were Catherine of Braganza, Sarah, Duchess of Marlborough, Addison, Cowper, Pope and Sheridan. Fanny Burney the novelist said it was: "a most delightful spot; the prospect is beautiful, the air pure, and the weather very favourable to invalids."

The Hot Well, though, was regarded in its time as a last resort when other treatments had failed; one set of lodging houses was known as 'Death Row'! All was not gloom, however; there was scandal and cards, an orchestra to listen to, boat excursions down the river - or across it to eat strawberries at Long Ashton. Or people could go up to the races on the Downs. Catering for almost every eventuality were three tailors, three wig makers, a milliner, a dressmaker, a laundress, a soapmaker and five shoemakers. There were three bakers, a brewer, three butchers, four grocers and seven medical men.

The water, in glass bottles made in Bristol, was sent all over the world, but the spa declined and in 1822 Hotwell House was demolished so that Bridge Valley Road could be built.

SOME ASTONISHING CURES
reported by Dr. Alex Sutherland in 1763.

Consumption: **William Darvise** of West Street, Lawford's Gate, Bristol, aged 53, at the last extremity of consumption, a frightful skeleton, continually coughing, straining and spitting day and night, his appetite gone, sleep vanished and his friends hourly expecting his death, by drinking the Hotwell water is restored to appetite and sleep, hale and active, without cough or any remaining symptoms. (Lucky old chap!)

Diabetes: **Mrs Hemming**, South Parade, Bath, aged 70, corpulent and tall, laboured under great thirst, parched tongue, fever and flux of urine, so that her strength was greatly impaired and her flesh much wasted. By drinking the water for one fortnight her tongue became moist, her urine lost its sweet taste and was reduced to its natural quantity. (Taste? Who tasted it? Yuk!)

Stone and Gout: **Mr Martin**, purser of a ship was afflicted with a diarrhoea for six years. He was also subject to gravelish complaints voiding great quantities of fabulous matter. (Fabulous? Well, I suppose you could call it that, at a pinch.) By drinking the water two months only he was completely cured of both ailments.

External Disorders: **Miss Lancaster** of Castle Green, six years old, had the King's Evil running at one finger, out of which came a bone, with a running in her left cheek, her foot and toes hard and cruelly swelled. [Poor little kid.] By drinking, bathing and medicines intermixed, she was cured.

[**Brilliant**, as her elder sister would say today!]

The Downs

Bristol's beautiful playground was preserved for the use of Bristolians for ever by an Act of Parliament in **1661**. Clifton and Durdham Downs were originally the commons of medieval manors, a wild, lonely place shunned by travellers after dark for fear of highwaymen and footpads.

In 16th Century Bristol St. Michael's Hill near Highbury Chapel had a macabre fascination for the townsfolk, for it was the scene of public executions, which always drew huge crowds. The condemned had to walk from Newgate to Cotham (though seafaring convicts were executed at Canon's Marsh, and their bodies suspended in an iron cage hung low over the water as a grim warning to the crew of every passing vessel.) Small children suffering from warts were often lifted up to be touched nine times by the hand of the executed criminal, and the rope with which they were hung was in big demand as a cure for ailments! In the mid-17th Century the bones of executed felons whitened in creaking chains on the gibbet at Gallow Acre Lane, where Pembroke Road now runs. As Clifton developed, so did The Downs. The Ostrich pub on Durdham Down did brisk business with customers who came to watch boxing, wrestling, cock-fighting or a race for maidens - the first prize for which was a lace Holland smock. These days the Downs give pleasure to people in their thousands, as season follows season.

Admire the lovers in the sun,
To be a'courtin' must be fun,
To walk and hold a loved-
one's hand
Upon the Downs, it must be
grand.

Bill West, Southmead, 1995

Colston (1636-1721)

Edward Colston owned a large fleet of ships, with which he imported sugar and other produce from the West Indies; mainly from St. Kits, where, at the time, there was extensive trafficking in slaves. He gave freely out of the immense profits he made, for example to Colston's School, the almshouse on St Michael's Hill, the Merchant's almshouses, Bristol Cathedral, St Mary Redcliffe.

The dolphin crest, worn by the Colston boys since 1776, is said to celebrate the providential escape of one of Colston's ships from wreck by the forcing of a dolphin into a leak which would have sunk the ship.

Among the conditions laid down when he founded the school were that the boys should: "Rise before six in the morning, and having dressed themselves attend prayers in the Schoolroom... and after reading some portion of the Scriptures and singing psalms their breakfast shall be given them and they shall enter school by seven. From thence at eleven to dinner, returning to school at one and continuing there until five, on Thursdays till three. On Saturdays Catechism after dinner and then free until seven. On Sundays matins in the Cathedral and Evening prayer in the Schoolroom."

For breakfast the boys had bread and butter, bread and broth or bread and gruel; for dinner bread and beef or hot bread and butter, pease pudding with butter, or bread and boiled mutton; for supper, bread and cheese.

In 1710 Colston became one of Bristol's two Tory Members of Parliament - until 1713. His charities, as far as they are known, amounted to £100,000 [nearly as many millions in today's money] of which he distributed £20,000 to the London poor in 1709, a year of famine.

He died a bachelor in 1721, aged eighty-four. The Colston Society, the Dolphin, the Grateful and the Anchor are all existing charitable groups which were set up after his death to commemorate him.

EDMUND BURKE

Being born in Catholic Dublin yet schooled in Quaker ways produced conflicting influences: he had a sharp Irish temper, softened by the caring attitudes instilled in him during his schooldays; he had the lucid intellect of a lawyer and the rhetoric of an actor. He was a Bristol Member of Parliament for six years (1774-1780) and though he did well for the city in many ways he fell foul of some of the greedier merchants and departed Bristol rather acrimoniously. He was the finest speaker in the Commons.

"**Edmund Burke**, 1729-97. Educated at Trinity College, Dublin. B.A. 1743. Qualified as a barrister at Middle Temple, London. Became private secretary to the Marquis of Rockingham, then MP for Wendover in 1765, renowned as "an orator of the highest class." MP for Bristol 1774-80, and for Malton 1781-94. Was unpopular in the House of Commons. Supported Wilberforce in his campaign to abolish slavery. During the impeachment of Warren Hastings (1794) spoke for **nine hours** ." [Phew!]

Concise Dictionary of National Biography.

Hannah More

Hannah Moore was born in **1745** in Fishponds alongside the church and died aged 88 in Windsor Terrace, Clifton. She was "kind, pretty and prim." Two plaques commemorate her: one where she lived, at 4, Windsor Terrace, the other where she worked, at 45, Park Street.

After a life of writing she became a social worker. She fretted about the appalling living conditions of the poorly-paid workers in the villages around Bristol and offered educational, spiritual and financial help to try to alleviate their poverty. She also campaigned against slavery.

The Wesleys

John **Wesley** (1703-91) first came to Bristol in **1739**. On 2nd April he spoke to about three thousand people in the Brick fields at St Philips Marsh, using the text "The Spirit of the Lord is upon me because He hath anointed me to preach the gospel to the poor... to heal the broken-hearted...and recover the sight of the blind, to set at liberty those that are bruised." He bought a piece of land near St James' churchyard in the Horsefair and three days later the first stone was laid of the building that was to become a Society Room, a meeting place. In 1759 he visited French prisoners of war (from the Seven Years War) in their camp at Knowle, after which he drew attention to their dreadful living conditions and raised support to alleviate them. It is estimated that John Wesley rode more than 200,00 miles around the country on horseback to deliver his message to people.

One of John Wesley's dictums was a harsh version of Spare the Rod and Spoil the child:

"Break their wills betimes, begin this great work before they can run alone, before they can speak plain or perhaps speak at all. Let him have nothing he cries for, absolutely nothing, great or small. Make him do as he is bid, if you whip him ten times running to effect it. Break his will now and his soul will live, and he will probably bless you to all eternity."

He also said:

I often wonder at the people of Bristol. They are so honest yet so dull, 'tis scarce possible to strike any fire from them."

This could have been because his congregation were
spellbound by his preaching -
or, perish the thought, were lulled into sleep.

Charles Wesley (1707-88) wrote many of his 7,000 hymns while living in Bristol, at 4, Charles Street, Stokes Croft. Five of the eight children of Charles Wesley and his wife Sarah Gwynne lie buried in the churchyard of St James' church in the Horsefair.

The brothers' system of Protestant faith was meant to eliminate the then existing abuses of the Church of England. Today, world-wide, there are more than 25 million adherents of Methodism, primarily different from the Anglican church in its system of administration.

I don't suppose the brothers would have approved of...

A private dinner in the 19th Century when the Mayor entertained 21 guests, including an Admiral and four Army officers, to a dinner at which they consumed 62 bottles of wine. The whole thing cost £2.37p per head, about £100 today. Contrast that with the fact that in 1831 a servant girl, Anne Reynolds, earned a shilling a **week** (5p) and her victuals for slaving all hours of the day and half the night in a cheap rooming house near Christmas Steps.

She could never have afforded...

A new and elegant post coach [that] will set out from the Lamb Inn, Broad Mead, and from the Swan with Two Necks in London, every Monday, Wednesday and Friday morning at 6 o'clock, and will arrive London and Bristol the next morning.

To make it more agreeable to those who engage the whole coach, the Company may sleep in any part of the Road they think Proper in that the coach arrives any time the next evening.

Fare from Bristol £1-8-0 from Bath £1-5-0.
Snell, Jane & Co.

Coaching

A letter to the Gentlemen's Magazine in **1754** described the London to Bristol road as "the worst public road in Europe". [How about the M4?] In order to raise money from tolls levied on road users between 1707 and 1743 the entire length of the road was turnpiked. But turnpikes were very unpopular. There was vandalism, as in 1734 when miners from the Kingswood Forest **destroyed all the gates between Gloucester and Bristol.**

Bristol and Bath were the first cities to have a Royal Mail run.

On 31st July **1784** the following announcement appeared in Felix Farley's Bristol Journal:

"Monday next the experiment for the more expeditious conveyance of the mails will be made on the road from London to Bath and Bristol: the letters to be put into the London office every evening before eight, and to arrive next morning at Bath by ten, and at Bristol at twelve o'clock (NOON) - the letters for London, or any places between or beyond, to be put into the Bristol Office before three and into the Bath Office every evening before six   o'clock, which will be delivered in London the next day"

It is possible to give the approximate times of the mail run: allowing for 19 changes of horse calculated at two minutes per change (later, the G.P.O. allowed five minutes for a change of four horses) arrival at the Swan with Two Necks in London was "well before 8 o'clock", giving an average over the route of just under eight miles per hour. So for 6d one could now post a letter in Bristol at 3.30 pm on Monday and the letter could be collected at the G.P.O, London on Tuesday morning. If a reply were written the same day and posted by 7.30 pm in Lombard Street the answering letter could be collected just before noon on the Wednesday from the Post Office in Small Street. Postage was paid by the recipient.

In **1835** the Bristol Mail left London at 8 pm and arrived the following morning at the Bush, Corn Street, at 9.03 am. [20]

The Old Vic

Nearly every building in Bristol's King Street is scheduled under the Act as an ancient monument. Some of them stand in shameful neglect and decay. Almost alone among them the Theatre Royal, built in **1766**, is renovated and decorative, and still fulfilling the original purpose for which it was built.

It is the oldest theatre in the nation. When it was built, King Street, adjacent to the docks, was the centre of the city's life and commerce. The merchants lived in their handsome houses on the other side of the road, or in the neighbouring Queen Square, named after Queen Anne.

Always, the theatre has had to struggle in an atmosphere of storm or stress, and, at the very outset, the idea of a permanent home of drama encountered the fierce opposition of the religious element in the city. 18th Century Bristol had waxed rich on the slave trade, and when public conscience was aroused it found its expression in an excess of Puritanism.

For the previous forty years there had been a small theatre in what was then the countryside, half a mile outside the town at the foot of Brandon Hill. Run by an actor by the name of Powel, who had been a leading man with Garrick at Drury Lane, this building had become too small for the growing theatrical interest of the town. (Chatterton spoke of this theatre as the "hut at Jacob's Well".) A plot of land was acquired in King Street and, despite vehement local protests a company of citizens was formed to promote the scheme. Chief among the organisers were Alexander Organ, who was subsequently to become mayor of the town, and Thomas Symons, a solicitor. They gathered around them forty-eight people, who each subscribed the sum of £50. In return, these donors each received a silver token which gave them the right to a seat at one performance of every play produced in the theatre. Other money was subscribed and eventually the theatre was built at a cost of £5,000. The foundation stone was laid on the 30th November 1764, and the theatre opened on 30th May 1766. James Patty was the architect and Michael Edkins the decorator. A gallery was added towards the end of the 18th Century and the highly decorative ceiling raised to meet it.

Garrick was present in the audience for the inaugural performance, and described the building as "the most beautiful theatre in Europe". Despite the interest that he showed, Garrick himself never played at the theatre; his is, therefore, practically the only classic name missing from the list of actors and actresses who have trod the boards of King Street. The roll call includes, among many others, the Kembles, Sarah Siddons, Kean, Macready, Irving, Forbes-Robertson, Ellen Terry, Tree and Sybil Thorndike.[21]

Across the cobbled street, a famous Theatre stands,
With spacious foyer built within the Cooper's Hall.
Overhead crystal chandeliers like myriad stars,
On purple avenues and columns shed their light.
Seated within the horseshoe hollow, gold and blue,
The audience, hushed and still, sees the curtain rise.
On stage a trapdoor, cunningly contrived
To make the wicked demon disappear at will;
Above our heads a thunder roll with wooden balls.
Gilded boxes, high-backed seats, crows nest up aloft,
Bridging two hundred years of playing on the stage.
Macready, Siddons, Garrick, phantom-like appear,
Parading still, familiar haunts of bygone years.

Noelle Wells, Bristol 1983

In the early years of the 19th Century the Theatre Royal was in parlous social and financial decline. When Dr. Wintle became its honorary physician, audiences were a rough lot, regaled by ill-paid touring players with such gems of over-acted melodrama as *Maria Marten, or The Murder in the Old Red Barn.* Once during a pantomime the doctor was summoned to examine the Principal (female) Boy, who had chest pains and a cough. On his arrival she was already in traditional Whittington costume. Asked to lie down *on the stage* for stethoscopic examination she refused, because she was wearing tights, which would split unless she remained standing. So a compromise was suggested: that she should gently lean back, legs outstretched, while he examined her. Bronchitis was diagnosed and she was advised to go immediately to bed, with a steam kettle in the room. [22]

A Flyer in 1736

Thomas Kidman, the famous flyer who has flown from several of the highest precipices in England, flew on Monday from the highest of the rocks near the Hotwell; with fireworks and pistols, after which he went upon the rope and performed several surprising dexterities on it in the sight of thousands of spectators.

The Weekly Miscellany, April 17th, 1736

There have always been what many people think are 'nutters'. Almost every day you can see breathless people clinging with broken fingernails and sweaty palms to the rocks of the gorge. On the 1st April 1979 four members of Oxford University bungee-jumped off the Suspension Bridge.

POPE'S EYE VIEW

Passing still along by the river, you come to a rocky way on one side, overlooking green hills on the other; on that rocky way rise several white houses and over them red rocks mixed with green bushes and of different coloured stone. This at a mile's end terminates in the house of the Wells . . .

When you have seen the hills which seem to shut in upon you, you go into the house (the pump room) and look out at the back door. A vast rock of 100 foot high, of red, white green, blue and yellowish marble, all blotched and variegated, strikes you quite in the face, and turning on the left there opens the river at vast depth below, winding in and out and accompanied on both sides with a continued range of rocks up into the clouds with a hundred colours, one behind the other.

Alexander Pope, letter of 1739

Chatterton

Thomas Chatterton was born in 1752 in the School House, Pile Street, near St Mary Redcliffe church, where his father was the schoolmaster. At the age of five he was sent by his widowed mother to be taught by his father's successor, but he seems to have made slow progress. [Thomas, not the successor, though it could have been both, I suppose.] Then a sudden change came: his mother showed him a manuscript in French with illuminated capitals with which he was so taken that he soon learned his letters from it.

In the Muniment Room at St. Mary Redcliffe, to which he was given free access, were ancient manuscripts which he read over and over again. In 1760 he became a pupil at Colston's School, and in 1767 apprenticed to Mr. Lambert, an attorney who had an office in Corn Street, opposite the Exchange. There he began to be trained as a scrivener, the duties of which consisted of copying out legal documents in a fair hand. It was about this time that he began to hoax the people of Bristol with his discoveries of "ancient documents".

Well aware of the prevailing interest in antiquities, in 1768 he sent to Felix Farley's Journal what purported to be an original account of the opening of Bristol Bridge in 1248, which was accepted as genuine. In time it, and other poems that he said were of ancient origin, turned out to have been written by him.

An extract from the "Tragedy of Goddwyn" gives an idea of the style and strength of Chatterton's poetry:

"When Freedom, drest in blood-stained vest,
To every knight her war-song sung,
Upon her head, wild weeds were spread,
A gory sword beside her hung.
She danced upon the heath,
She heard the voice of death.

Power, with his head stretched into the skies,
His spear a sunbeam and his shield a star,
Like two flaming meteors rolls his eyes,
Chafts with his iron feet, and sounds to war.

She sits upon a rock;
She bends before his spear;
She rises from the shock,
Wielding her own in the air.

Hard as the thunder doth, she drives it on,
Wit, skilfully disguised, guides it to his crown;
His long sharp spear, his spreading shield is gone;
He falls, and falling, rolleth thousands down.

In time, such poems would have brought him renown, but Chatterton was too impatient to wait for fame to come to him. He went to seek his fortune in London.

What happened when he got there has been differently interpreted. Some say that he was so poor that he took his own life in desperation. Others say that even at the time of his death his income was adequate. Yet others, that he took drugs. Whatever the reason, he committed suicide, aged only seventeen. It has been said that Chatterton was "difficult, spiteful, disagreeable and his own worst enemy." Be that as it may, there is no doubt that his early death took away a special person who might have gone on to give us very special poetry.

A monument erected to him in 1840 on the north side of St. Mary Redcliffe Church, shows him in the uniform that he wore as boy at Colstons School.

Sale of forger poet's letter to Walpole

A LETTER by an 17-year-old poet to Horace Walpole, the 18th century dilettante, will be auctioned in London on Thursday. The letter was written by **Thomas Chatterton**, who was ostracised after forging poems he claimed were by the 15th century Bristol monk Thomas Rowley. Walpole was held partly responsible for the boy killing himself with arsenic in 1770, aged 17, after the fakes had been revealed. Chatterton had written to Walpole, 4th Earl of Oxford, enclosing the fake poems. At first, Walpole offered "a thousand thanks", but he returned them after being told by the poet, Thomas Gray, that they were forgeries.

Chatterton's reply, dated April 8 1769, is expected to fetch up to £7,000 at Christie's. He said he had copied Rowley's poems "from a Transcript in the Possession of a Gentleman who is assured of their authenticity".

Jane Flower, Christie's manuscripts specialist, said: "The outrageous charge that Walpole had driven Chatterton to suicide did much to damage his reputation."

The Daily Telegraph,
26th June 1995

A BUSY CITY

In 1724 there were twenty sugar refineries in Bristol processing imports from the West Indies. There were also fifteen glass factories, turning out great quantities of bottles that were filled with water from the Hot Wells. Millions of pins were also made in Bristol, to meet the demand from busy seamstresses, and tons of soap - mostly, in those days, used to wash clothes and not to clean bodies. In 1750 the first porcelain to be made from Cornish clay was made on Castle Green.

Account of disturbances at The Lamb, Lawford's Gate

DECEMBER 18th, 1761, hearing that Mr. Giles's children, Mifs Molly and Dobby, were afflicted in an extraordinary manner, for a fortnight past, I went there this day, and saw Molly sewing; and found she had marks on her arms given on a sudden, like the marks of a thumb-nail; which I am satisfied she could not do herfelf. As I watched her, I faw the flesh pressed down and rise again, leaving the print of a finger-nail, the edges of which grew red afterwards. The girl complained that it came with the force of a finger, hurted her much, and smarted after. I inquired of Mr. Giles, when this first took place; he said, " On Friday the 13th of November last, the children being all in bed in the morning, something scratched violently at the window and bed's-head, and they were so frightened, that they jumped out of bed and ran down stairs."-As nothing of this kind occurred till about three weeks afterwards the father and mother thought it was the pigeons that had made a noise at the window.

Thursday the 31st my sister and I went in the morning and saw some of the prints of the fingernails; heard a little clawing on the ground and saw Molly's head beat against the window with great force. We were told how the great table was, by an invisible force, turned quite upside down, twice in an hour in the presence of three persons. Mr.....saw a chair move from the wall and fall down. Mr....was sitting in the room with Mr Giles and others and saw the poker and shovel rise from the chimney and be thrown to the other end of the room. A key that was hanging up came five yards and struck Mr Giles on the head.

Tuesday the 5th I went at eight in the morning. I heard a rolling over my head which they said was the chamber pot, as usual, rolling around the room whilst the children were at prayers, which many have seen.

Monday the 29th, Molly the maid felt a cold hand flap across her eyes!

As all these commotions continued above the year people were determined to go to the *cunning woman* at Bedminster, a White Witch, to see if she could stop it. They did, and she bid them to take the children's first water in the morning and put it in a pipkin on the fire and if, when it boiled, all colours of the rainbow came out visibly she could cure it.

They accordingly put the water on the fire and, several told me, beautiful colours came out, like the rainbow. From that day there had been no disturbance; but have been quiet above a year.

How far the cunning woman contributed to this I will not pretend to say.

By the late Mr. Henry Durbin, Chymist
Who was an eye-witness to the principal facts herein related. (Never before published)
R.Edwards
Broad Street, Bristol, 1800

"SHIP-SHAPE AND BRISTOL FASHION"

The earliest reference to this saying is from Scott's Chronicles of Canongate, of **1829**:

"When we set out on the jolly voyage of life, what a brave fleet there is around us as, stretching our fair canvas to the breeze, all 'ship-shape and Bristol fashion,' with pennons flying and music playing, we. . . "

Statue of Charles Wesley.

HANNAH MORE

FRED LITTLE

Colston
the great
benefactor

Burke
the great orator

77

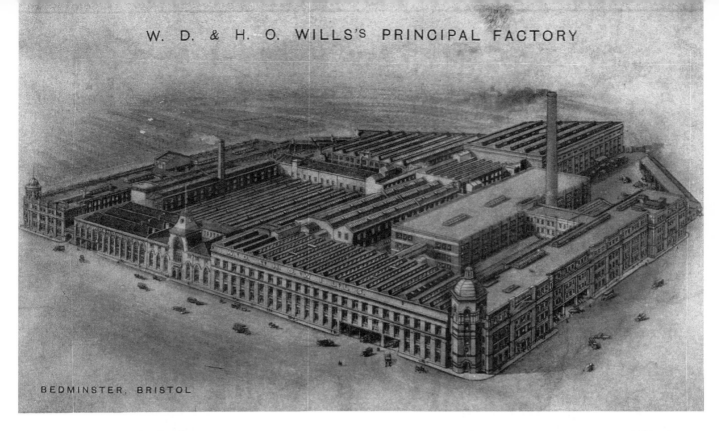

BEDMINSTER, BRISTOL

Christmas decorations in the Wills factory, 1885

TRAMWAY CENTRE, BRISTOL

BRISTOL TRAMWAYS & CARRIAGE C? L?

St Mary Redcliffe

More Famous Bristolians

Robert **Southey** (1774-1843) was born in Bristol, in Wine Street, where his father was a linen draper. In **1795** he and Samuel Taylor **Coleridge** were engaged to be married to two sisters named Frick from Westbury-on-Trym. Coleridge was married on October 4th, and Southey on November 14th, both at St. Mary Redcliffe. Coleridge went first to live at Clevedon, but returned to a home on Redcliffe Hill for a short time in 1796. Southey went for time to Portugal, and on his return spent a happy year at Westbury. "Never before or since" he said, "have I produced so much poetry in the same space of time." He was in constant touch with Coleridge and the scientist Humphry Davy during this year, for they often met as guests of John Wedgwood, brother of the famous potter, at Cote House, Westbury.

Man hath a weary pilgrimage
As through the world he wends
On every stage, from youth to age,
Still discontent attends;
With heaviness he casts his eye
Upon the road before,
And still remembers with a sigh
The days that are no more.

Southey, *Remembrance*

And, seemingly in contradiction...

You are old, Father William, the young man cried,
And pleasures with youth pass away,
Yet you lament not the days that are gone:
Now tell me the reason, I pray.

Southey, *The Old Man's Comforts*

Oh what a wonder seems the fear of death,
Seeing how gladly we all sink to sleep!

Coleridge, *Monody on the death of Chatterton*

As idle as a painted ship
Upon a painted ocean,
Water, water everywhere,
Nor any drop to drink.

Coleridge, *Rime of the Ancient Mariner*

The famous novelist and poet, **Charles Kingsley**, went to school in Bristol. He was taught by the Rector of St. Michael's who described him as "affectionate, gentle, and fond of animals".

He did not know that a keeper is only a poacher turned inside out.
The Water Babies

Life is too short for mean anxieties.
Saint's Tragedy

Humphrey **Davy** was born in 1778, and lived in Penzance. At first his interests were mainly concerned with literature, but when his father died in 1794 and he became assistant to an apothecary in order to supplement the family income, he studied to become a doctor. He was particularly interested in experiments with the new gas Nitrous Oxide, or "Laughing Gas". When only twenty years old, he came to live at 3 Rodney Place, Clifton. Here he soon made the acquaintance of Coleridge and Southey.

In 1801, before he was 23, Davy became Assistant Lecturer at the Royal Institution. Within ten weeks he was Professor there, and was soon launched on his great discoveries in electricity and metallurgy. However, he is best remembered for the invention of the miner's safety lamp.

The historian, **Macaulay**, also resided in Bristol for some time, at 16 Caledonian Place, Clifton. In his poem, "The Spanish Armada," he makes special reference to Bristol in the lines:

**"Right sharp and quick, the bells all night rang out from
Bristol town,
And 'ere the day, three hundred horse had met on Clifton
Down."**

Bristol Corporation

Both before and after the Municipal Reform Act of **1835** there existed a Corporation of Bristol consisting of the Mayor, Aldermen and Council. Up to 1835, the Council was known as the Common Council and was a closed body filling vacancies by co-option. After 1835, the Council was known as the Town Council and its members were elected by the ratepayers.

Taxation

Bristol's local taxation in **1833** amounted to £**100,000**:

Poor rate	£30,000
Paving & Watch	14,500
Church	2,000
Dock & Harbour	26,200
Cranage, etc.	4,000
Town and Mayor's	2,800
Miscellaneous fees	20,500

The total was sufficiently large to provoke concern about its magnitude. Alarm among ratepayers was expressed more about the size of the impost than about suspected waste or misspending.(16)

Now have a look at your Council Tax!

Patrick O'Brien, **the Bristol giant** born in Ireland, stood about eight foot four in his outsized socks. But he was a gentle giant and never raised his leg-of-mutton sized fists in anger. One of his pleasures was to light his pipe by raising the lids of street lamps!

He died at Hotwells on the 8 of September, **1806**, in the 46th year of his age. The inscription on his tombstone read: "Here lie the remains of Mr. Patrick Cotter O'Brien, a native of Kinsale, in the kingdom of Ireland. He was a man of gigantic stature, exceeding 8 feet 3 inches in height, and proportionably large. His manners were amiable and unoffending, And the inflexible integrity of his conduct through life, united to the calm resignation with which he awaited the approach of death, proved that his principles were strictly virtuous.

The leaden coffin in which he was enclosed measured nine feet two inches, and the wooden case four inches more. (It was born by **14** pallbearers.)

He was buried with all decent privacy "near the stairs of the Romish chapel; the time a profound secret, probably in the night, to avoid as much as possible the gaze of the vulgar. To prevent any attempt to disturb his remains, of which he had the greatest horror, a grave is being sunk to a depth of 12 feet in the solid rock, and such precautions taken as would effectually render abortive either force or stratagem."(24)

FRENCHAY
NATIONAL
SCHOOL

On 18th April 1842 Hannah Rooke donated half an acre of land on Frenchay Common "For the purpose of establishing a school for the poor persons of the parish and the residence of the schoolmaster and school-mistress.'

It did not become law to have to keep a school log until 1865 and we do not know much about the school before this time. The 1851 Census names the National Schoolmaster as Charles Price, 23, who lived in the schoolhouse with his wife Martha and daughter Eliza.

From June 1865 Mr Alfred Stokes, the Headmaster, kept a regular log of school life. The log notes the establishment of a 'shoe club' so that the poor could save up for new shoes; the fact that the school gate was left open and horses got into the school grounds, and so on. A recurring concern of his was the absence of a school clock and bell. At this time the only clock available to poorer people was the church clock, most homes having no clocks or watches. He frequently refers to it in his log - probably to draw it to the attention of the local gentry who visited the school.

1865, 7th November. We are sadly in need of a school clock.

1866, 13th February. Experience great difficulty in adhering to the school timetable in consequence of there being no clock.

7th May, Trees now being thickly covered with foliage, the clock on the church tower cannot be seen from any part of the school grounds and we are therefore sadly put to an inconvenience as to time, having no clock.[25]

The Mansion House

Each year the councillors of the city of Bristol elect their civic leader for the next twelve months. The first mayor took office in 1216, and since 1899 the position has been dignified with the rank of Lord Mayor. Less than thirty cities in the United Kingdom have the privilege of styling their civic head in such a way, and only the sovereign - in Bristol's case, Queen Victoria - can bestow the honour.

For their year of office the home of the Lord Mayor is the Mansion House on the Promenade at Clifton Down. Of the 1,000 or so functions attended by the Lord Mayor during the year of office, around 100 are held at the Mansion House.

The present Mansion House is the third official mayoral residence. The first was an early-18th Century house in Queen Square and was occupied in 1786. It was burnt down in 1831 during the riots. A temporary replacement was found in Great George Street but that was shut down when the reform of municipal corporations decreed that official residences were not needed.

The Mansion House, on the Promenade, Clifton Down, cost £2,500 in 1867, has twenty-two rooms and was built of stone quarried on the spot. (The area around the Downs was dotted with quarries in the boom years of Victorian building, especially the rock faces of the Avon Gorge.)

In **1874** Mr. Proctor decided to give the house to Bristol, on 1st May, his wedding anniversary.

The Lady Mayoress' badge.

The City's Further Development

As the 19th Century entered its third decade, Bristol continued to expand, both in physical extent and in population. Medieval Bristol, the seventeen original parishes centering on the fork between the river Frome and the old course of the Avon, was now, relatively speaking, only a shrinking nucleus of the built-up area. Admittedly, recent growth had transformed St. Michael, St. James, St. Paul and St Augustine into populous parishes. Yet even they were being over-shadowed by Clifton's development as a fashionable suburb and Bedminster's new role as an area into which the working class was migrating. The central city, infested with dank, dark lanes, was no longer capable of containing the thrust of commercial demands and the grander aspirations of many inhabitants. In two decades Bristol's population rose by over 20,000. Between 1801 and 1811 this upsurge gave Bristol's numbers a greater boost than any other provincial town except for Birmingham, Liverpool and Manchester. By 1821, Bristol was on the verge of containing 100,000 people.

Bristol's economic transition was less spectacular. In the 18th Century, thanks chiefly to the wealth which shipping, West India sugar and slaves had brought, prosperity had almost come to be taken for granted. Until the advent of the 19th Century or even beyond, this feeling seemed justified; the port was the most advantageous terminal of the main routes from Africa and the West Indies, and the city's commercial interests were diversified. But ships were getting bigger and the harbour was too shallow.[5]

William Jessop, a pioneer of civil engineering in Britain, had already achieved a national reputation before he was consulted at the beginning of the 19th Century on proposals to improve the harbour facilities at Bristol.

The result, in **1809**, was that by damming the Avon at Rownham and redirecting its course from Totterdown through the New Cut, enough permanent high water was provided for the existing quays and for the creation of many new quays around what was now called the Floating Harbour. Ships were no longer stranded on tidal mud when the tide ebbed.

It was confidently expected that the Floating Harbour would revive the prosperity of the port, but despite later improvements and additions, such as the extension of the Canon's Marsh wharves and the building of large tobacco bonded warehouses, trade contracted; large iron ocean-going ships which began to come into service after the 1840s could not make the journey up the Avon. Bristol's decline was only halted by the construction of the new, bigger docks at the mouth of the Avon, the first of which were completed in 1877. Two years later other docks were built at the river-mouth at Portishead.

The port of Bristol is the only major seaport in Britain to remain under municipal control. [26]

Isambard Kingdom Brunel

Important Dates

1829	A competition announced for a new bridge over the Avon Gorge at Clifton; won by I. K. Brunel.
1833	Great Western Railway Co founded; I. K. Brunel engineer.
1836	Foundation stone of Clifton Suspension Bridge laid 27th August.
1837	Steamship *Great Western* launched on 19th July.
1840 1864.	Work halted on Clifton Suspension Bridge. Completed Jan
1843	Steamship *Great Britain* launched on 19th July.
1858	Steamship *Great Eastern* launched on 31st January.

Throughout the length and breadth of England it would be hard to find a landscape so well calculated to appeal to Brunel's romantic temperament, to his love of drama and his sense of grandeur, as the fantastic gorge which the Avon has carved through the limestone escarpment which barred its way to the Bristol Channel. The precipitous crags of white limestone, capped by the little observatory; the black maw of the Giant's cave adding a suggestion of Gothick gloom; the admirable foil of Leigh Woods, thickly clothing the Somerset slope opposite, and lastly, far below, the silver skein of the tidal river bearing to Bristol Port the shipping of the seven seas: here was every ingredient that his fancy could desire. It is easy to imagine his excitement when he heard of the proposal to bridge the Avon gorge and to invite engineers to submit designs. Here indeed was a project after his own heart. Let him design a bridge worthy of such a setting, a triumphal arch that would leap from lip to lip of Bristol's seaway in one sheer and splendid span.

Brunel decided that the site called for a suspension bridge. He visited the Menai and devoted two days to a minute examination of Telford's bridge...he also visited the Scotswood and Stockton suspension bridges. In his diary at this period, too, he pasted a cutting of a newspaper account of the collapse of the Broughton suspension bridge near Manchester: the rhythmic tread of a company of troops marching over the bridge had set up such a violent harmonic motion that a pin in one of the suspension chains broke and the bridge collapsed at one end.

The span of a suspension bridge all is lightness and aerial grace; its strength resides in the suspension towers and anchorages which uphold it. To make this strength manifest and thus to point the contrast between the opposing towers and the slender web of links and rods they bear, Brunel's native adaptation of an ancient monumental style was a stroke of artistic genius. Every line of these squat towers which straddle the roadway with firm-planted feet is eloquent of their purpose, a purpose admirably emphasised by the simple monoliths of stone atop the chain anchorages.

On June 18th 1831 the Bridge Committee decided to commence work by clearing the site on the Clifton side and on the 21st a very odd little ceremony took place. While workmen began digging on Clifton Down a public breakfast was held at the Bath Hotel, after which the gentlemen and their ladies walked to the site, where they assembled in a circle round a pile of stones which had been dug out. Brunel then entered the circle, picked up a stone from the heap and handed it to Lady Elton who, holding it in her hand, made a short speech. This was followed first by a deafening discharge of cannon which had been mounted on the rocks just below and then by the distant strains of the National Anthem, played by a band of Dragoon Guards who were down in the gorge. Colours were then run up on a flagstaff erected for the occasion while Sir Abraham Elton delivered the usual flowery oration. "The time will come," he said, turning to Brunel, "when, as that gentleman walks along the streets or as he passes from city to city, the cry would be raised 'There goes the man who reared that stupendous work, the ornament of Bristol and the wonder of the age.'" This provoked loud cheers, and the toast "Success to the undertaking and to the conductor" was drunk in sparkling champagne, the "humbler citizens being regaled with a barrel of beer".[5]

The SS Great Britain

When Prince Albert had launched her in 1843, with a length of 322ft and a displacement of 3,675 tons, the Great Britain was then the largest ship afloat - and the first of that scale to be built of iron. She was the first liner to be screw-driven (though with schooner-rigged sails on her six masts). She was also equipped with the first watertight bulkheads, the first virtual double bottom and the first balanced rudder.

The top of the huge chain-wheel which drove her propeller projected through the deck, where it was housed in a special compartment. The Great Britain could achieve 12 knots, and in 1846 made the crossing from New York to Liverpool in 13 days. That September she ran aground in Dundrum Bay, Co Down, and was not refloated for nearly a year. The owners were ruined, but the disaster showed that iron ships could survive where wooden ones would break up.

After various modifications (including the reduction of the masts to three) the Great Britain gave some 25 years' service on the Australia run, carrying as many as a thousand passengers at a time. She was also used as a troopship in the Crimean War.

In 1882 her engines were taken out and her hull clad with pine, after which she began a new phase as a sailing cargo vessel. Four years later, battling westwards round Cape Horn, she lost her top-masts and had to put back to the Falkland Islands. For 50 years she was used as a storage vessel in Port Stanley harbour, until in 1937 she was towed out to Sparrow Cove, where she was holed and beached. By the end of the 1960s she was close to breaking up.

Goold Adams was alerted to her plight in 1968, when he saw a photograph in a newspaper. Within a few months he had become chairman of the Great Britain Project, which undertook feasibility studies and the raising of funds. The work required enthusiasm and slog in the face of myriad disappoint ments and could only have been undertaken by someone with a private income.

Jack Hayward, a property millionaire, agreed to meet the cost of bringing the ship back to Britain. In 1970 the salvagers succeeded in manoeuvring the Great Britain on to a pontoon and towing her 7,000 miles back to Britain. On July 19th - the 127th anniversary of her launch - the Great Britain returned to the dry dock originally made for her construction.

The Bristol City Corporation seemed less than delighted by her reappearance and unanimously resolved to make no financial contribution towards her restoration. Goold-Adams pressed on undeterred, and in 1975 the corporation agreed that the Great Britain should remain in the Great Western Dock at a pepper-corn rent. By 1982, when Goold-Adams surrendered the chairmanship of the project the hull had been largely restored.

Goold-Adams was appointed CBE in 1974. He died aged 79.

From an Obituary in *The Daily Telegraph*, May 1995

VOYAGE 47

The present dies - like music - in the moment of creation;
Through its narrow door the future slips away.
The years that make us older
Spirit everything away; sand castles crumbling in the tides
Of long ago; a century whose mighty fleets
Have sailed away for ever. Someone else's world
Becomes involved in the machinery of Time
With its iron slowly rusting
Like the gentle death of Autumn.

...

Great Britain, now a veteran, embarks on voyage 47,
Only to be battered in a roaring seascape,
Limping to a distant port, abandoned by advancing years.
Life goes on in music halls, in gaslight and the groaning trams.
Dolls all over England go in mourning for a dignified old lady
Wearing diamonds in her bonnet. Clocks go ticking on into
Another century. Great wars arrive to drink the blood of nations.
In Falkland's isles the iron castles come and go
Like thunder in a hill of clouds.

...

Now, high and dry above her ancient ways, gradually
Forgetting water, silent as a dream, she stands, a stranded ark
Transmitting our humanity. As after storms light rainbows down,
So does the towering spirit shine of those no longer in the world,
The lively dead. Thus from her deck I see again the bible gaze
Of all her captains sailing over a sea of creatures,
Transversing the ages as though nothing lay between and all
The outspread years were drawn together; for who can tell - perhaps
In some foreverness all that has existed still exists and we may be -
Like this great ship - harbouring a secret immortality.[10]

The SS GREAT WESTERN

Historically, the first voyage of the Great Western is of unusual interest. Having seven passengers on board, she started on April 8th, 1838, astonished a liner "seven days out from Liverpool," by-passing her on the third day from leaving Bristol, and berthed at New York after a voyage of 15 days and 10 hours, the return voyage (with sixty-six passengers,) taking only 14 days. Instead of the 1,980 tons of coal which had been asserted the vessel would have to carry, she took less than half that quantity, and only 450 tons were actually consumed. At New York so great was the importance of the event that 100,000 people were present to witness her departure for England.

SS Great Eastern

The ship, named Leviathan at her launching, left Liverpool on September 10th 1861 for New York under the command of Captain James Walker. Three days out she encountered a storm of such severity that a heavy sea carried away one of the boats on her weather side. Swinging at sea level from one of the davits it was in imminent danger of fouling the paddle wheel, so Captain Walker ordered the ship astern, so that the boat could be cut away without risk. Taken unawares by this sudden manoeuvre, the helmsmen lost control of the wheel with the effect that the huge rudder, sucked by the screw, swung over until the quadrant hit its stop with such a mighty jar that the vertical steering shaft broke clean in two at its weakest point - just above the ball-bearing which carried its weight. The great ship immediately fell off and lay broadside at the mercy of the storm.

From the stern of the crippled ship there came a terrifying succession of detonations as the useless rudder beat itself against the blades of the screw. The engines were stopped. The ship might still have been manoeuvred on her paddles but such was the fury of the seas that in a very short time nothing remained of the two great wheels but the bare hubs, and the ship was left completely helpless. She rolled so heavily that her grand saloons were practically wrecked before the crew managed to regain control of the rudder with jury tackle.

The cost of repairs was such that the ship had to be sold, and was then used for cable laying. On the last day of June, 1866, to the music of "Goodbye, Sweetheart, Goodbye" from the band of the guardship, and resounding cheers from ships and shore, the great ship swung slowly away from her mooring at Sheerness with her cable tanks full.

On the 26th July the Great Eastern steamed slowly into the inlet in Heart's Content Bay, Newfoundland, and on the following day, amid scenes of wild enthusiasm, the cable was taken ashore by the tender Medway. "The old cable hands seemed as though they could eat the end" wrote [an engineer by the name of] Gooch; "one man actually put it into his mouth and sucked it. They held it up and danced round it cheering at the tops of their voices. It was a strange sight. I am glad two of my boys were present to enjoy and glory in their part of so noble a work. They may, long after I am gone, tell their children of what we did." Gooch then sent through the cable the news of their triumph: "Gooch, Heart's Content to Glass, Valencia, July 27th, 6 p.m.: Our shore-end has just been laid and a most perfect cable, under God's blessing, has completed telegraph communication between England and the Continent of America."

For the first time, the new world spoke to the old.

As a result of this success the Great Eastern went on, like some industrious spider, to weave a web of cables round the world; from France to America and then from Bombay to Aden and up the Red Sea. (3)

*

The Clifton Suspension bridge, the highest single suspended span in the world, is undoubtedly one of the most beautiful ever constructed. It stays youthful because its classic lines will always appeal to the eye. It does, however, hold a dreadful fascination for people who are mentally troubled or in despair.

Suicide on the Bridge

A man survived with a few broken bones after falling 245ft from Clifton suspension bridge in Bristol yesterday. The 36-year-old man was pulled from the banks of the Avon by emergency service crews after bridge workers lowered a ladder to the river's edge and hung on to him. It is not known if the man jumped or fell. He was conscious throughout and complained of feeling cold when paramedics arrived to treat him.

Pedro Noya and Clint Badlam were replacing light bulbs when they heard shouts that a man had fallen in. "We threw a harness to him and tried to comfort him," said Mr Noya. "It's amazing that someone could fall all that way and live. Me, I've always been afraid of heights."

Paramedics crawled across the mud on mats to the man, identified only as "Chris", and put a neck collar on him. He was then strapped to a stretcher and hoisted from the bank by a Fire Brigade crane. He was taken to Bristol Royal Infirmary, where X-rays showed he had suffered fractures to a leg, arm and collar bone. His condition was said to be "stable."

The bridge has been the scene of more than 1,000 suicides since it was built. In 1993 Angela Stratford, a 29-year-old sports mistress from Gwent, dissuaded a suicidal engineer from jumping by talking to him for an hour. [Some reports said three hours.]

Concerns about the number of deaths - around one a month - led the Samaritans to install telephone hotlines at either end in 1991, but bridge trustees ruled out fencing in the walkway or placing nets underneath to prevent suicides.

Amazingly, over the years eight other people have survived
falls from the bridge

SOME WHO LIVED TO TELL THE TALE

Sarah Ann Henley, a 22-year-old barmaid, threw herself off the bridge in 1864 but was saved when her billowing skirt acted as a parachute. She lived to the age of 85.

In 1896 Birmingham tradesman Charles Brown threw his two daughters off the bridge but Elsie, 3, and Ruby, 12, were rescued after a strong wind and high tide helped break their fall. In 1991 a woman broke her back when her fall was cushioned by bushes. She made a full recovery. In 1992 Anadan Ganesan, 19, a student, walked away from his jump without breaking a bone. He later collapsed with internal bleeding on the towpath.

The Daily Telegraph, 31st May 1995.

And, of course, there's the Great Western Railway, another monument to the genius of the little man with the big cigar and the even bigger stove-pipe hat.

In 1833 business men in Bristol promoted the idea of a railway from London to Bristol. In 1835 an Act of Parliament authorised it. By 1838 twenty miles of track were laid and two years later the railway reached Bristol, cutting through Box Tunnel on the way, itself a great feat of engineering.

The journey took three to four hours but was distinctly unpleasant for the Third Class passengers. "The ends and sides of each vehicle extended a bare six inches above seat level, with the consequence that, when facing a strong head wind, in addition to concentrating his attention upon retaining his hat, a passenger was obliged to be extremely careful lest a sudden jerk might prove fatal in its unbalancing effects," as a passenger of the times wrote.

In 1841 when the GWR services between London and Bristol began, "Bristol time" was still **10 minutes later** than London time.

96

Cholera

In **1849** cholera came to Bristol. There were 778 cases, of which 444 resulted in death. A health report later commissioned by the Council stated that:

There were no sanitary authorities in Clifton, in which lived an estimated 60,000 people, or in St. Philip's Parish, Westbury or Bedminster. Sixty-four people were living in **one** house in one of the stench-filled Courts during the epidemic.

Sewage from houses in Kingsdown ran down to St. James and sometimes into the dwelling houses. Some sewage drained into cess pools which filtered into nearby wells.

Whiteladies Road had an open gutter for sewage. Clifton was poorly lit, whilst Bedminster, Redland and Cotham had no lights at all. Ashes and house refuse was thrown daily into many private roads in the suburbs, and never removed. Drunkenness, filth, and excessive mortality were attributed to want of drainage and want of water.

In 1851 a new law gave the council power to make the necessary improvements. When cholera came again in 1866 there were only 29 fatalities.

And another opinion of Bristol,
after it had been cleaned up!

Sir John Betjeman, former Poet Laureate, who stayed in Clifton for a few months when he was a boy and visited the city often thereafter wrote:

"There is no city in England with so much character".

"It is the most beautiful, interesting and distinguished city in England."

REPORT

of the

Bristol and West of
England Society
for
Women's Suffrage
1873

**OBJECT - To obtain for
women
householders
and Ratepayers the
right of voting for
Members of Parliament**

BRISTOL :

**H. HILL, STEAM PRINTER,
2 BALDWIN STREET.**

1874

An Eminent Bristolian

THE RIGHT HON. SIR EDWARD FRY,K.C., P.C., J.P.,G.C.M.G.

was one of the most distinguished members of the family so long associated with Bristol.

After a brilliant career at the Bar and on the Bench, he ably filled the high office of one of the Lords Justice of Appeal, from which he retired a few years since on a well-earned pension, and has since lived in the neighbourhood of Bristol as a country gentleman, where he often sits on the Bench of Magistrates at Long Ashton Petty Sessions, to the advantage of his colleagues and the public in general, and has frequently been called upon to deal with important matters entrusted to him as arbitrator; besides on several occasions delivering instructive addresses on some of the important matters of interest to the community.

In appearance he is a slight, well-built man, of grave, dignified aspect, unassuming and unaffected, very courteous and amiable in manner and disposition, respected and esteemed far and wide as a man learned in the law, who freely gives to his fellow creatures the benefit of his life-long experience, and spends the evening of his days in honourable retirement, but is still willing to give a helping hand to any good objects which may appeal for his influence and support. Consequently, his opinions are always received with much appreciation on local or Imperial matters, when expressed at public meetings or appearing in print, dealing with any of the popular topics of the times.[27]

And, in Contrast, a Worthy Cabbie

My grandfather rented out a hansom and a four wheeler, had his place in a stand in St James' Barton but did quite a lot of extra business with funerals and weddings. Like so many typical Bristolians he was not a Bristolian, but had been born the son of a gentleman's coachman and a chambermaid outside Bath, though he probably grew up in Bristol.

He was basically a respectable man; hard-working, conscientious, a good family man in a heavy Victorian manner, often slightly under the influence of brandy and hot water or snatched rums between fares on winter nights - a hazard of the trade - but never noticeably drunk. He talked affectionately to my grandmother in a very Bristolian way, ticking her off with mock-testiness, talking wistfully of his next wife, muttering "I'll 'ave to 'ave thee shot", being rude to her relatives or his own if they stayed too long by ostentatiously taking his boots off and dumping them in the hearth to warm for the morning. But there was a close bond between them and she waited in the dark front room behind the curtains for him to return from a late fare.

He was devoted to his horse, which he also grumbled at but never neglected. Sometimes, if he was tired or too full of brandy or rum, he would leave the cumbersome cab outside in the street all night, unharness the horse, lead it through the carriageway to the stable at the back of the house and put it to bed - or through the hall and kitchen if the man who rented a stall in the stable had thoughtlessly left his cart blocking the carriageway!

He was a great wag, known and liked in a wide area of the city. He died at 49, probably worn out by the irregular life and over-exposure.(28)

[And the brandy, perhaps?]

Samuel Plimsoll

It is appropriate that his bronze bust can be seen a few yards from the water at Hotwells. He was a fearless campaigner much of his life and no-one did more to make the seas safer for sailors. He is dubbed 'the Sailor's friend', an unofficial title he earned by taking on the ship-owning interests in often bitter confrontation. His birthplace was 9, Colston Parade and he spent early working days as a solicitor's clerk and the manager of a local brewery. He was elected M.P. for Derby and his outspoken style of oratory was apt to get him into trouble. Once he had to make a public apology in the Commons.

The improvement of safety standards at sea was his agitating preoccupation. He was shocked by the scandal of overloaded cargoes and he successfully fought for a compulsory load line on ships - the Plimsoll Line. He remained a paassionate pamphleteer after his parliamentary days and died in 1898. A plaque can be seen at the Bridge Head, to the left of Neptune's Statue, facing down river.(29)

WG Grace

was only fifteen when he played for Bristol against an all England XI on the Downs. England lost by an innings; he contributed 32 runs to their defeat. He and his talented brothers, E.M. (The Coroner) and G.F. (Fred) dominated Gloucestershire cricket for years.The Champion, as he was called, captained England and Gloucestershire, scored 126 centuries and took as many wickets with his distinctive round-arm deliveries. He was arrogant and pig-headed but amazingly skilful.

The Wills Family

Henry Overton Wills, the father of W.D. and H.O., founded the tobacco company in 1786. It began production in a dwelling house; in time it employed over ten thousand people.

Over the years the family has been extraordinarily generous in its charitable gifts to many different causes.

101

BLOODSHED

There have been six serious riots in Bristol. In **1709** the price of wheat rose from 4/- to 8/- a bushel, and over 200 colliers from Kingswood entered the city and rioted, joined by some of the poorer citizens. They dispersed only when promised that the price would be reduced to 5s6p a bushel. In **1714**, on the accession of George I, the rabble of the town took the side of the Tories, and roughed up Whigs and Dissenters. When special judges were sent to try the offenders, fresh disturbances broke out. Owing to this, and events of a like nature in other towns, the Riot Act became law. In **1753** another bread riot broke out; colliers and others caused an affray which cost four lives. Many people were injured.

The Bristol Bridge riot occurred in **1793**. The new bridge had been built by commissioners who were allowed to repay themselves by levying tolls on all traffic using it. After 26 years of tolls the commissioners had over £2,000 in hand, and demands were made that the tolls should cease. It was promised that the bridge should be free after 29th September, but a few days before this date the tolls were again advertised for sub-letting. A mob gathered on 28th, burned the toll-gates, and pelted with stones the magistrates and militia who arrived to preserve order. Next day, a Sunday, was quieter, but trouble began again on the Monday. The magistrates called in the Herefordshire militia and read the Riot Act, and then ordered the soldiers to fire. One man was killed and several wounded. The mob reassembled and began to destroy the toll houses and their furniture and the militia were again ordered to fire, when eleven persons were killed and forty-five wounded.

And 1831

The Background

The riots of 1831 were one of the most dramatic episodes in the history of the United Kingdom: more people were killed and injured and more damage was done in Bristol than ever occurred anywhere else in the kingdom before or since.

The upheaval was a manifestation of bitter resentment against an unfair system; a sudden release of frustration by a growing population who were becoming more literate and politically aware as time passed. However, during the disturbances there was not, as there had been in the French Revolution, a blood lust that called for the death of those who were thought to have created the conditions that led to the frenzied outburst; even at the height of the uproar, when men, women and boys were surging around with their emotions inflamed by passion and alcohol, the very people they were protesting against went about their business with very little molestation. Unplanned, chaotic, violent but not vicious the riots started spontaneously as a protest and then got out of hand as the wilder spirits realised that they were unfettered; that there was free liquor to be had and loot, but also, and perhaps of more importance to them, that for once in their lives they could say exactly what they thought and do exactly as they pleased.

Early in **1831** Lord John Russell had introduced his Reform Bill in Parliament, but it had been defeated. Later in the year another Bill was introduced by Lord Grey, passed the House of Commons, but was rejected by the Lords. One of the most prominent opponents of the Bill in the Commons had been Sir Charles Wetherell, Recorder of Bristol, and when it became known that he was to arrive in the city on 29th October to open the Assizes, the mob gave him a rousing reception. His carriage was pelted with stones, especially by the women of Temple parish, and although the court was opened, there were violent interruptions. An adjournment followed during which Sir Charles was driven to the Mansion House in Queen Square to the accompaniment of howls of derision.

It was soon evident that the Recorder's life was in danger. The 14th Light Dragoons and a troop of the 3rd Dragoon Guards, under the command of Lieutenant-Colonel Brereton, were summoned, to find all the windows of the Mansion House broken and the mob busy tearing down the railings and prising up the paving stones. The Riot Act was read, but Brereton refused to fire on the mob unless given signed orders by the Mayor, which responsibility the Mayor refused to undertake. The Recorder made his escape in disguise over the rooftops of adjoining houses, and later so did the mayor, dressed, so it was reported, as a washerwoman. [Shades of Toad of Toad Hall!]

Eventually, Brereton led the Dragoons into Queens Square, where they drew their swords and laid about the people. The exact number of deaths during the riots is not known, but estimates ranged around the five hundred mark. Fifty-one buildings in Queen Square were destroyed, together with toll-booths, prisons, the Customs House and the Bishop's Palace.

At one point during the riots I.K. Brunel went down into the city from Clifton, where he had been convalescing after an illness.. "Went to the Mansion House," he wrote in his diary. "Found it nearly deserted. It had been broken into again and sacked." He dashed into the building and with the assistance of two other men carried silver and pictures over the rooftops into the Custom House.

The Trial and Death of the Colonel

The Court Martial which tried Lieutenant-Colonel Brereton for dereliction of duty in his handling of the riots assembled at ten o'clock on the morning of the 9th January 1832.

The trial took place in the Great Room of the headquarters of the Society of Merchant Venturers in King Street, near the Broad Quay. Along the length of a large table down the middle of the room sat the fourteen officers who were members of the Court, while at the head of the table sat the President, Lieutenant-General Sir Henry Fane, and the lowly Captain, Thompson, of the 81st of Foot, who had been appointed Deputy Judge Advocate. All of them, except Lieutenant-Colonel Forster of the Royal Artillery, wore scarlet; he was in blue, with heavy, gold-braided epaulettes. Many of the officers wore campaign medals from the Napoleonic Wars

To the left of the President, at a separate table, sat the accused, also in scarlet but with a high blue "choker" collar embellished with silver piping, which was also sewn in twisted cords across the front of his tunic. He had brown hair, and a good head of it; cut short and not swept back, it fell across his forehead in a way that could not have changed much since he was a boy.

The charges were read to the prisoner; to each Brereton stood and replied "Not Guilty."

The court met each day of that week, hearing the evidence against the accused, and adjourning each evening, when Brereton was allowed to go home.

On the fifth day, Friday the 13th at two o'clock, the court reassembled and, their names having been called over, the President immediately stood and said "You will probably have heard a most distressing report relative to the prisoner. I have sent Major Mackworth and the District Surgeon to ascertain the facts and if you please we must wait to hear the report of these individuals."

Shortly after this Major Mackworth entered the room "covered in dirt". The President then addressed him: "Major Mackworth, in conformity with the order you received have you been to the house of Colonel Brereton?"

"I have."

"Was he dead or alive?"

"He was dead."

The Court was then cleared. "It had not been so crowded, throughout the whole of the Court Martial, particularly with ladies," wrote the reporter from the Bristol Mercury.

The next day, a Saturday, a Coroner's Inquest was held at the colonel's house. The "very respectable" jury were sworn in and immediately went to view the body of the deceased. The Proceedings of the Inquest recorded that "A more harrowing spectacle could hardly have been conceived. The body was lying extended at full length on the bed, with the head upon the pillow and the mouth and eyes open. The right arm was stretched close by the side and the left, the one with which it is supposed the fatal act was committed, was in a raised position, bending backwards towards the shoulder. The pistol was on the floor, close to the bed. The body was partly undressed, the coat, waistcoat, stock and boots having been taken off. Every one present seemed impressed with feelings of pity and regret."

Mrs Ann Pitchforth, the first witness, said she had been housekeeper to the deceased for about sixteen years. The last time she saw him alive was at two o'clock on Friday morning. He had returned home at about eleven but did not retire to his bedroom for some hours. She had heard him walking about for some time. It had always been his custom to kiss and say goodnight to his children ere going to bed, but he did not do so that night, a thing which he had never omitted do before. The deceased went to his room about two o'clock and about fifteen minutes later she heard a pistol shot. Being much frightened she waited for a few moments and then going into the bedroom found the deceased lying there. His state of mind had gradually got worse since Monday last. There was no-one in the room when the occurrence took place. (This witness was in tears while giving her evidence and on retiring from the room, fainted.)

While the Inquest was being held the two orphan girls, "who were most interesting children", according to the reporter from the Mercury, were to be observed looking through the cottage window, apparently unconscious of the grievous bereavement which they had suffered.

One of the letters written by Brereton during the hours when he alternately paced about or scratched at parchment with a quill was addressed to his uncle, Lieutenant-Colonel Andrew Coghlan, who lived in Bath. It read: "My ever dearest uncle, My unfortunate mind is not now in a state to enter into particulars and I can therefore only hope yourself and dearest aunt will not forsake my innocent and helpless babes. Do not let poor Pitchforth want, she has been a faithful creature to me. I cannot say more. God in heaven bless you both." The letter was later accepted as being his only Will, and on 2nd April his uncle was granted administration of it, and the guardianship of the two girls.

A small cortege departed from Redfield House at seven in the morning on the following Thursday, but many hats were doffed and many heads were bowed as the coffin passed, and "a considerable number of the populace" joined the principal mourners as the procession moved through the streets on the long journey up to the crypt of Clifton Parish church, where the colonel was laid to rest beside the remains of his wife.

But even in death Tom Brereton was not to find peace, for on the night of 24th November 1940 one of many German bombs dropped on Bristol destroyed Clifton Parish church. The repair of the shattered city naturally took priority over less important matters and due to a wartime shortage of labour it was decided that the crypt in which his body had been buried would be filled in and covered over with turf.

He lies somewhere under the grass, surrounded by the bones of many genteel Bristolians, at the top of a hill from which there is a long view over the city in which the rabble lived in their hovels.

The Hangings

His Majesty's Commission for the trial of the Bristol rioters began on Monday, the 2nd of January 1832. In the course of the preceding week the Sheriffs had sworn-in nearly all householders in the city as special constables, more than two thousand of them. In addition to the sizeable force thus created a body of men were also formed for the protection of the Judges. These, under the control of Mr Dowling, were dressed in a uniform similar to that worn by the Metropolitan Police, while the specials were identified by the name of their parish or district, printed on calico or card and placed in their hat band or pinned to their jacket.

At half-past ten the Judges' coaches, each drawn by four greys, were seen approaching from Bath. Amid a flourish of trumpets the lawmen were handed into other carriages provided for their reception and, "with not a single indication of disrespect being apparent", made their way to 6, Park Street, where they donned their robes of office. Then, in state, led by the City Swordbearer wearing his fur hat - Ye Cappe of Maintenance - and carrying the Lent Sword, preceded by the Mayor and followed, draggle-tailed, by the Corporation, they solemnly processed to the cathedral to hear Divine Service.

The trial then followed, day after day, at the end of which five men were convicted of a capital offence.

On Thursday, the 12th January 1832, they were brought up to receive sentence: Christopher Davis, Joseph Kayes, Richard Vines, Thomas Gregory and William Clarke were placed at the bar. After the judges had donned their black caps the prisoners were asked in turn if they had anything to say regarding why sentence of death should not be passed. When it came to Kayes' turn he fell down in a fit of agony and his convulsed frame had to be restrained by six men. Writhing around he shouted "Oh, I'm not guilty! I'm not guilty. Oh, my God! My wife, my children!" By order of the Lord Chief Justice he was taken back to the cell below, but for a considerable time his ravings could be heard in the court and created a great sensation. Gregory turned to address the court in broken sentences, saying "Oh, my dear Lord, I am innocent; as innocent as a child unborn. Oh, have mercy on me, my dear Lord!" The others remained silent.

On Friday the 27th of January, fifteen days after sentence had been passed and despite a petition to the King signed by ten thousand Bristolians, "including several merchants of the greatest respectability", Davis, Clarke, Gregory and Kayes were hanged over the entrance to the ruined New Gaol. **[The gate still stands, beside the canal.]** Only the day before, Vines, the youngest of the five, had been told that his sentence had been commuted to perpetual banishment, on the grounds that he was an idiot, and that he was to be sent to Australia.

A great number of spectators, thousands of them, subdued, still and silent, had taken up their positions on the opposite side of the Cut, waiting in a bitterly cold wind for the appointed hour of noon. However, it was after one o'clock before the prisoners were led out - preceded by the Reverend Day reading the burial service - whereupon there was a great sigh of sympathy. People murmured such things as "There's Davis, unfortunate fellow," and "God save us, there's the poor lad Clarke". A great number of them, including many of the special constables, began to weep.

On the scaffold Gregory was placed on the left, then Davis, then Kayes then Clarke. Ropes were put around their necks and a white hood was placed on their foreheads. They then embraced each other and kissed each others' hands, the hands of the Divines who attended them and the hand of Governor Humphries, who also shed tears.

With each of them expressing a strong belief in the hope of eternal happiness Gregory stood like a soldier on parade; the others remained still. (The previous April Davis had attended the execution of a man found guilty of burglary and when it was over had turned to the friend who was with him and exclaimed "It is horrible! God only knows who will be next".) Clarke, when his turn came to have the hood drawn down over his eyes, begged for a moment of time and then bowed three times to the crowd. Each in turn then forgave the executioner, who was a poor, dirty, ragged and wretched-looking person who had taken the job as a desperate means of earning a few pennies. While he was fixing the ropes around their necks he shook so violently that to prevent him from falling off the scaffold one of the jailers had to hold him but, clawing at the shoulders of Kayes and Gregory to steady himself, he eventually completed the task and with a trembling hand pulled the lever.

In the middle of their prayers the four voices of the condemned men were suddenly cut off by the jarring crash of the platform as it gave way under their feet. They plunged down and then their bodies hung, swinging gently from side to side, like grim exclamation marks, in front of the silent, bare-headed and aghast crowd. Except for Kayes, who twitched and writhed for several minutes.(30)

The sixth occasion of rioting was, of course, that in St Paul's in 1980, which was basically racial in nature. People of many races and creeds live in Bristol, giving the city a rich mixture of talents - but also sometimes leading to tensions.

In the summer of 1983 the Lord Mayor held a reception in the Mansion House for the ethnic minorities in Bristol, thinking that there were perhaps ten or a dozen different groups in the city. It turned out that there were **fifty-two:** Africans, Chinese, Cypriots, Greeks, Estonians, Indians, Lithuanians, Latvians, Pakistanis, Russians, Ukranians, Vietnamese, West Indians, and so on, nearly all of whom had some sort of central point of contact in the city to which they gravitated for mutual support and friendship. And there were also, of course, many expatriate people from European nations living here: French, Dutch, Italians, Belgians... As well as Americans, Australians, Canadians... You name them, they're nearly all here.

Though it has not yet reached the centenary of its foundation, Bristol
University is firmly established as one of the nation's leading institutes
of learning. After Oxford and Cambridge, Bristol University, together
with Durham, is the one that would-be under-graduates would most
like to attend. The Wills' tower dominates busy Park Street, at the
heart of the city.

The Roman Catholic Cathedral in Clifton is one of the most renowned examples of modern church architecture in the country. Its majestic soaring external lines are in contrast to the tranquillity of the interior, with its space and quiet colours.

A water-colour painted by H. O'Neill around 1821 showing the Limekiln Lane glasshouse. In the 1830's it was shut down but by then another glassworks had been established in Nailsea.

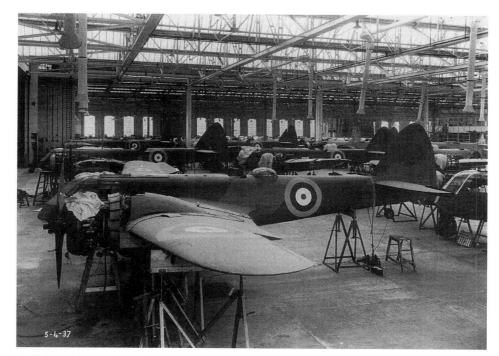

Bristol Blenheim bombers being constructed at Filton during World War 2. Below is the Brabazon, a white elephant as it turned out, because jet engines overtook the piston-engined concept of the big plane, but a milestone in its way. One that, in time, led to Concorde.

For the men at the front World War 1 was an indescribable horror; for the women at home it was wrapped in sentimentality. In truth it is appalling everywhere, as the people of Bristol found in 1941.

WILLIAM CLARKE.

CHRISTOPHER DAVIS.

Contemporary portrait sketches of the four men who were hanged after the riots of 1831

THOMAS GREGORY.

JOSEPH KAYES.

Fullers coach works produced splendid high-class carriages in the
18th and 19th Centuries. Bristol cars maintain the same standard of
excellence in the 20th, building cars of outstanding originality.

Glass Making

Glass making had been an important industry in the Bristol region since its establishment in the 17th Century. Although pieces of Bristol glass produced during the 18th and early 19th Centuries are now prized collectors' items, originally glass manufacture concentrated on bottles and window glass. In 1722 at least fifteen glass houses flourished in or near Bristol, but their numbers declined until by 1833 only four survived.

Glass making was a highly skilled occupation, with whole families involved in the trade.

"**Nathaniel** Warren is a tall slender man, about 20 years of age 5 feet 8 inches high, with a small face, dark complexion, black eyes, thin straight black hair and a scar near one eye occasioned by a cut. He had on a dark blue coat with yellow buttons, a yellowish striped velvet waistcoat, a pair of olive coloured velvet breeches and a fashionable round hat.

Robert Warren, his brother, is a genteel-grown well-looking lad of about 15 years of age, 4 feet 3 inches high, with a round smooth pale face, dark straight hair and black eyes. He had on a dark claret coloured coat, no waistcoat, a pair of corduroy breeches and a round hat.

Joseph Dully is a shabby, thin, slender, lank-jawed, herring-gutted lad of about 16 years of age, four feet four inches high, with pale complexion, grey eyes; is grown out a small matter in one shoulder and carried his head leaning over the other. He had on a dark claret coloured coat, no waistcoat, a pair of black cloth breeches and an old brown flopped hat.

[Weren't they well dressed?]

In **1792**, Hannah More, evangelical philanthropist and founder of Sunday Schools, visited the glassworks with her sister Patty, who described it in this way:

"We now made our appearance, for the first time, among the glass-house people and entered nineteen houses in a row (little hovels) containing in all nearly two hundred people. Both sexes and all ages were herding together, voluptuous beyond belief.

The work of a glass house is an irregular thing, uncertain whether by day or by night, not only infringing upon a man's rest, but constantly intruding upon the privileges of the Sabbath. The wages high, the eating and drinking luxurious - the body scarcely covered, but fed with dainties of a shameless description. The high buildings of the glass houses ranged before the doors of these cottages - the great furnaces roaring - the swearing, eating and drinking of these half-dressed, black-looking beings gave it a most infernal and horrible appearance. One, if not two, joints of the finest meat were roasting in each of these little hot kitchens, pots of ale standing about, and plenty of early delicate-looking vegetables...

From the cottages, which exhibited the usual scene of filth, feasting and gross ignorance, we proceeded to enter the very glass houses, amidst black Cyclopean figures, and flaming, horrible fires. However, we were again agreeably surprised as well as affected, for everyone of these dismal looking beings laid down their tools, calling all the great boys out of their black holes, and using really persuasive language to them to induce them to listen to us and do what we wished..."

Being highly paid, the glass workers could afford a good diet. Sometimes there were "one or even two joints of roasting meat and plenty of early vegetables" on the table. Snails were eaten partly as a delicacy and partly as a means of allegedly combating chest diseases. A man called John Eyres said of the practice: "As long as you get the right kind of snails, in dry condition, they are very palatable. I have eaten and enjoyed them myself, baked upon a shovel held for a few minutes at the mouth of the furnace, and taken from their shells with a two inch nail. If oysters, mussels and winkles, why not snails?"

[Ah, well, it's all a matter of taste.]

The lads, usually apprentices, had to arrive before the men to make preparations for the day's work, and so worked on average 13 or 14 hours in each "journey". There were seven "push-boys", who pushed the cylinders of glass into the kilns where they were flattened out by the men.

"They work from 6 till 6, days one week and nights the other, except on Mondays and Saturdays. On these 2 days, the 2 sets work less, dividing only 18 hours between them viz. from 12 on Sunday night till 6 a.m. on Monday, and on Saturday from 6 am until 12 p.m. They usually have no work on Wednesday night.

Boys were not allowed to take another boy's shift, since they would be too tired, and if a boy broke even one piece of glass that would be as much as a good bit of his wages. Indeed, in all parts of glass house work, the principal things was to have a good supply of hands.

Apprentices aged between 13/14 and 17/18 helped by carrying the pipes, holding them at the furnace and some, known as spare boys, held shovels at the furnace to screen the gatherers from the intense heat. Boys pushed glass into the flattening kilns. Boys should not be apprenticed younger than 12, with 14 as the upper limit, but they needed to have been in the glassworks for some time before this. Boys were essential to work at night with the men. The minimum age for the founders crew was 18. In 1841, 25 young boys were employed but this had risen by 1862, to 50 under 18 out of a total work force of 200.

Glass making was thought to be a healthy occupation and many workers lived to a ripe old age. As someone recorded ".. all the men who are thus engaged in the very hottest departments in our works are remarkably healthy. One of them is now about 70 years of age and is still healthy although he has been engaged in the arduous duties nearly 50 years."[31]

Wages Paid at Nailsea 1836/7

Annually
Managers	£200
Clerk	£100 (+ allowances worth &20)

Weekly
Potmaker	35s. (+ house and coal)
Furnace Mason	28s. (+ house and coal)
Headsman	28s.
Assistant	12s.
Lad	7s.

Horfield Barracks & Prison

In order to avoid having to quarter troops on publicans in the city, as had been the usual practice - talk about asking for it! - Horfield Barracks was built in the mid-19th Century at a cost of £57,000 - which today, as we all know, won't even buy a first-time buyers' semi. For some time the barracks was the Depot of the Gloucestershire Regiment. It existed into the 1960s.

Nearby, Horfield Prison was built in **1873** at a cost of £120,00, which brought an outcry at the expense, since at that time there were only 150 prisoners in it....

Meanwhile, another form of discipline was being exercised at...

CLIFTON COLLEGE

The boys in the dormitory [1879-85] of which I had part-charge were older and bigger than myself. Many of them were distinguished in the various fields of athletics and by no means unconscious of their eminence; with these boys I had scarcely a bowing acquaintance.

It was one of my duties to impose a period of silence, so that they should say their prayers; but most of them were quite devoid of prayerful inclinations.

My requests for silence were not received politely; in fact, I might as usefully have addressed them to the lions and tigers who could be heard roaring in the Zoo a few hundred yards away. But, gentle reader, imagine your-self a youth of eighteen or nineteen, who has spent part of the live-long summer day patriotically compiling a century for your School against Cheltenham or Sherborne, and then imagine yourself, at the close of that great day, being ordered to pray by a small, obscure boy who is not even in the House Eleven! Would you not think him presumptuous ? Would you not feel like Prince Henry when he was " run in " by the Chief Justice?(32)

The Death of Queen Victoria

According to the *Clifton Chronicle* on 30th January 1901, "Signs of mourning are universal. Every social function has been abandoned and numerous events postponed."

The death of Queen Victoria came as a great shock to the nation at a time when respect for and veneration of the monarchy was perhaps as great as it has ever been. In the city centre on the day of the funeral, 2nd February, nearly everyone was dressed in mourning. On College Green wreaths were solemnly laid on her statue.

Chaos in the Gorge

On Sunday morning, 12th May **1878**, the schooner Gypsy became stranded in the Avon Gorge and effectively blocked the river passage to all but the smallest vessels, bringing the port of Bristol to a virtual standstill.

The Gipsy, a regular visitor to the port, had arrived with a cargo of livestock. After loading a general cargo she left just after midnight, towed by the tug Sea King. The two passed under the Clifton Suspension Bridge at about three o'clock in the morning and when she reached the point known as "Black Rock", the Gipsy struck the rock and mud on the Bristol bank. Fortunately, her bow was only a few feet from the shore and the one passenger on board was quickly helped to safety, followed by the crew. She listed over to one side and entirely blocked the river.

When the news spread, people in their hordes came to view the disaster. By the afternoon, when tugs tried to move the stranded ship, the crowds were said to be in their thousands; many had swarmed onto the Avonmouth railway line, which afforded the best view. According to the local press "loud shriekings from approaching engines were necessary to warn the public of their danger". The spectators were given a wonderful free entertainment, if such a term could be used.

When the tugs failed to move the vessel, a steam fire engine was brought by open barge to pump out the water before the crew could start unloading the cargo. Then at about eight o'clock in the evening there was a loud report like the discharge of a cannon, caused by the steamer parting in two, or, as it is familiarly known, breaking her back. Immediately upon this the men made a rush to leave the steamer but it soon became known that there was no real danger and they remained on board and pursued their task.

It was decided to use dynamite to remove the Gypsy and an expert from Glasgow was called in to supervise the operation.

Even by mid-week the vessel was still causing intense public interest. Thousands of spectators tramped through nearly three-quarters of a mile of mud.

There was a veritable hive of activity to observe, with 500 labourers engaged in taking the Gypsy apart and over 200 navvies widening the channel by removing the bank on the opposite side of the river. [The word 'navvies' was a shortening of the word 'navigators', which is what the labourers working on canals in the 18th and 19th Centuries were called.] By the Thursday, part of the river was open to small craft but it was several weeks before the channel was completely free. The last charge of dynamite was laid on 4th June. A young lad was injured by flying metal, though he was standing some 400 yards away from the scene. Even three weeks after the accident there were still plenty of onlookers.

*

It would be another 51 years before a similar disaster struck the port and this one proved to be even more spectacular. On 1st November 1929 no less than seven vessels of various sizes became stranded in the river. Two large steamships, Bristol City and Sappho, had left Bristol docks, while at the same time and on the same tide the Peursam and the New York City were coming up river. Then thick fog suddenly came down, reducing visibility to barely a couple of feet; the various masters and pilots were helpless, incapable of guiding their vessels. It was said that all that could be heard was the frantic and shrill sounds of the ships' sirens and loud crunching noises as vessels hit one another before becoming stranded on the mud-banks.

As the tide started to ebb the full enormity of the scale of the disaster could be seen. The Bristol City had virtually turned full circle and her bows were pointing back along the river from whence she had come. The Peursam had grounded close by and as the tide receded she slipped slowly down the mud to come to rest finally on the Bristol City. The steamship New York City had been stranded slightly higher up the river; although her rudder was put out of action she was re-floated on the next tide and towed back to Avonmouth. All the vessels were moved and within 24 hours the channel was opened again to shipping. By some miracle not one life was lost on any of the stranded vessels or on the numerous salvage tugs that came to assist. (34)

THE SOCIAL WHIRL

We are glad to perceive that Lady Horatia Webbe Weston and Lady **Ida Waldegrave** have taken No. 16, Caledonia Place for a short time. We hope these ladies, who are members of the illustrious house of Waldegrave, and the many other nobility who are wintering among us may find the fashionable watering places of Clifton sufficiently agreeable to think of making it their permanent residence. [A modern Waldegrave, William, the MP for Bristol West, lived for a time in what in 1857 was considered a slum - Wellington Terrace. Some places have gone up in the world, some down.]

Clifton Chronicle, June 1852

A SMALL TRAGEDY

On Saturday morning the body of an infant was discovered, wrapped in an old newspaper, lying in the path from the Observatory to Clifton Down.

Clifton Chronicle, 1856.

And Another

Mary Ann Rogers met a dreadful and untimely death under deplorable circumstances when at 4 p.m. her clothing caught fire when a poker fell out of the coals onto her and set her alight.

Clifton Chronicle, 1861

The Medical Profession Moving with the Times

"I am happy to say that I have never vaccinated anyone and am of the opinion that such a wicked and cruel and unnatural practice should be prohibited by act of Parliament.

A doctor, writing to the Clifton Chronicle, 1886

Bristol Zoo

The zoological society was founded on September 18th, **1835**. Founder shares were taken up by some 220 "proprietors". (The only benefit for a shareholder was free admission to the gardens, including Sunday, when the public was excluded.) The list of subscribers contained famous names - familiar now as streets in the vicinity - such as Beaufort, Worrall and Tyndall. Other names were Fry, Wills, Brunel and Charles Pinney, the last being the Mayor who escaped the fire [in the Mansion House in Queen's Square] at the time of the Bristol Riots in 1831.

The zoo gardens opened on 11th July **1836**. They comprised about twelve acres of farmland with a cottage - and a lime kiln, which would become the site of the bear pit and the present aquarium. **At that time the area was in the countryside and Gallow's Acre Road, now Pembroke Road, was a muddy lane running up to the site of the gallows.** Nearby was the tollgate house for the road running down from Clifton to Hotwells. The present School House of Clifton College was a public house, "The Carpenters Arms". (In 1862, twenty six years after the zoo was founded, Clifton College was opened across the road and has proved a friendly and helpful neighbour ever since.)

Associated entertainments included children's rides on the elephant and camel, and in the llama and goat carts; boat trips on the lake, roller skating, ice skating on a flooded area in front of the bandstand (erected in 1891), tennis, croquet, golf and archery, and many concerts were held. In view of Bristol's present association with hot-air ballooning it is interesting that as early as 1859 balloon ascents were made from the zoo. There were fetes and flower shows, bands played and acrobats, singers, conjurors and dancers performed. Visitors came by steamer from Chepstow, Newport and Cardiff, and by excursion trains from Stroud, Cheltenham, Gloucester, and Taunton. The cliff railway running from the side of the Grand Spa Hotel down to Hotwells was in use at this time and in the zoo prospectus of 1894 a trip to and from the zoo via this railway, followed by the tram from Hotwells into the Centre, was recommended.

A zoo entertainment for the Whitsuntide holidays in 1858 was:

"A Colossal Representation of the Siege, Storm, and Capture of Delhi. The greatest event which has distinguished the brilliant operations of our noble European Army in India against the Sepoy Mutineers and their traitorous leaders. The principal feature of the siege - the Blowing Open of the Cashmere Gate - will be represented by a highly-effective Tableau Vivant. A brilliant Feu de Joie, representing a discharge and counterdischarge of shells, closes the storming incidents of the siege."

These days the zoo requires vast quantities of food. In the course a year the animals consume 30 tons of meat, 15 tons of fish, 15,000 loaves of granary bread, 11,000 pints of milk, 10,000 cabbages, 700 cases of apples, 300 cases of bananas and 600 bags of carrots. (35)

*

And another

"I went to the stage and found a performance was going on. There were comedians, nice tarts singing and dancing, one with a baby in her arms, another was dressed like a black negro queen in short skirt and headdress of feathers. Then a fellow came on playing musical instruments, mandolin, bells, harp etc. Next a big overgrown schoolboy in mortar board, jacket and collar, doing a lot of larking. It was a puzzle how they done it. Next there was a little fellow performing tricks on a bicycle, dressed like an 11th hussar he mounts his bicycle and makes a grand charge. I went round by the lake and seen a man climb up on a wire over the water. With pole in hand, he walked along it and either by accident or design tumbled off. Then I goes touring all the houses seeing the various animals. I strolls about, had smokes, and a lot of nice dotlets were dancing to the band, playing kiss in the ring. When it got dark they had displays of fireworks and sent up a balloon ".(36)

A Military Funeral

At the end of the 19th Century a large number of soldiers were stationed in Bristol. There were barracks on Horfield Common, at Hotwells and at Kelston. During the year **1893** these regiments, or elements of them, were based in Bristol or visited the city:

Royal Scots Greys
Dragoon Guards
Gloucester Hussars
North Somerset Yeomanry
Grenadier Guardsmen (How many, I wonder?)
A Highland Regiment
Inniskilling Fusiliers.
Prince Alberts Somerset Light Infantry
Gloucester Artillery
28th Regiment RA
75th Field Battery R.A. from Trowbridge
Devon and Somerset Engineers

Guardsmen, Scotsmen, Irishmen, the lot. The pubs must have done a good trade.

William Henry Bow, who lived in Strouds Place, was 28 years old when he kept a diary which recorded his daily life as an undertaker's assistant. The following entry is a graphic account of a military funeral he witnessed.

Fri Jan 13th, **1893**

Something unexpected happened this day, for as I was up by Lee's, I seen a detachment of the 28th Regt. from Horfield march by with officers & sergeants, and set I wondering what was on. After I had been waiting about there half hour or more, I seen them come past again & found it was a military funeral and rather a fine turn out also.

The 28th men were walking in front, in two lines with rifles reversed, next the hearse with sergeants walking by it & then a mourning coach. In the rear more people, and three soldiers of the Regt of Inniskilling Fusiliers in bearskins like the guards. I followed along down Union St., The Barton, up Stokes Croft. A fine afternoon it was. With other people I kept along with it up Cheltenham Road and then all up the Gloster Road to the top, and got up to Horfield Church at 3.30. Soldiers forms up in line by the gate leaning on the butt of their rifles, and six sergeants, shoulders the coffin which was covered by a Union Jack, headed by two clergymen, and followed by the mourners. They took it in the church, and some drummer of the 28th was there, and a good many people went into the church. I took a seat there with them, and seen the service out with organ playing.

Then out they comes to a grave close by the road where the firing party was drawn up, and the coffin was directed by Old Prince. The sergeants lowers it down & the parson read the service while all the people stood by, then at the word of command the soldiers all loads up, fires three volleys in the air over the grave, which they did smartly indeed, and made a fine scene there. I looked on with interest. When it was all over I had a look into the grave with others, came out, and seen the 28th form up to return. I went along with them on the march, up to the Barracks, and down to the gate, and seen em march in and dismiss. Also seen a couple of the Dragoon Guards there, and a Scots Highlander in kilt and plaid. It was the first military affair for the year what I've seen, good biz. Then I left the barx & starts back in a fine sunset and I done a regular forced march down the track.

Sat Jan 14th

I found a notice in the papers about that military funeral yesterday. It was Mr James Robinson, late quarter-master of the 61st Foot, Veteran of the Punjaub and Indian Mutiny Wars, and at the siege & capture of Delhi. So that is interesting to note and I'm glad I seen it.

*

THE BRISTOL SAVAGES

The Red Lodge in Park Row, where the Savages hold their meetings was built in a corner of the garden of Sir John Young's Great House in **1585**. Later the widow of Lord Byron bought it. Then from 1854 Mary Carpenter used it as the first Girl's Reformatory in England.

The Savages are so called because at an early meeting of the group of founder artist members, some of whom were deaf and shouting at each other, the Chairman told them during a heated argument they were behaving " like a lot of savages."

The Club was established for artists and art lovers. "We paint pictures; after that we create music and poetry for ourselves and for the many who come to encourage us by their presence", as one of the members once put it.

The group began in a small way in **1894** and a variety of meeting places were used before they moved to the Red Lodge and built their "Wigwam" in its garden in 1920. It belongs to the Corporation but the upkeep devolves to a large extent on the Savages. There is a treasure house of interesting objects in that historic building in Park Row.

At the first Annual Dinner of the Bristol Savages, held on 19th May 1904 at the Cafe Royal in High Street, with Brother Savage Wilde Parsons in the chair four shillings bought a dinner of: Anchovies or Herrings; Fresh Salmon and Cucumber; Grilled Steak and Onions or Forequarter of Lamb; New Potatoes, Spinach; Asparagus in plenty; Caviare on Toast or Soft Roes; Cheese; Coffee.

An Edwardian Father

My father was born in 1888, the offspring of an uneducated labourer and illiterate mother. As a child I tried to teach my grandmother the letters of the alphabet, but she was barely able to make a round letter 'O'. In spite of this I cherish the possible illusion that she did not lack intelligence. My father was born into a family of eight children, three of whom died in infancy.

The quality of life in their poor country cottage would be unimaginable today. A labourer's wage would not support his family above the poverty level; and when a considerable proportion, as in my grandfather's case, was spent on drink, the children's diet was barely adequate They were sent to school, each with a penny batch cake, their food for the day.

On his father's death he became a dock worker. In the years before the First World War there was much unemployment; before the advent of the Welfare State life for the unemployed was harsh. Those wishing to find work on the docks were obliged to attend at five o'clock in the morning. Some of the men unable to find work would cycle from farm to farm during harvest time. Here, in exchange for their labour, and in addition to a small wage, they would receive bread, cheese, onions and liberal quantities of home made cider. They often ended up falling off their bicycles, sometimes into the canal, on their way home. I heard the story many times of two of these labourers, who told my father that at the end of a day's harvesting they had each drunk twelve pints of cider. "And dost thee know if we'd a'wanted we could've 'ad a bellyful."

My father was an active member of the local swimming club and in the summer of 1911 decided to swim across the Severn from Sharpness to Lydney, a difficult feat owing to the strong tide and treacherous currents in the river; one of the fastest flowing in the world. He was accompanied by a small boat, the Mary Ann, with a companion, Bertie Goodman, aboard. Bertie, by virtue of being a dwarf, was a well know local character, and was chosen for his knowledge of the river.

My father dived off the pier and landed on the other side about half an hour later, to cheers from his supporters on both banks. The event was celebrated at a Dance and Social evening, when, during an interval between waltzes, lancers, veletas, two-steps, schottisches and various other entertainments, he was presented with a gold chain and medal commemorating the occasion.

In October 1917 he was awarded the Military Medal while serving with the 107th Field Ambulance. The citation stated that "This N.C.O. displayed great coolness and gallantry under heavy shell fire in connection with the evacuation of wounded from the aid post near the Forest D'Houthulst to the Advanced Dressing Station. His services throughout the day have been of the greatest assistance to the wounded." In 1918 a Supplement to the London Gazette dated April 17th read, "His Majesty the King has been pleased to award the D.C.M. to the undermentioned for gallantry and distinguished service in the Field." Here his number, rank and name were followed by "For conspicuous gallantry and devotion to duty during operations. He has been in charge of stretcher bearers for a long period and always displayed great courage and initiative in collecting and evacuating the wounded. He set a magnificent example to all with him."

My father...taught me the names of the wild flowers, and knew just where to find the different ones as they bloomed. In the spring I came home with bunches of primroses cowslips, bluebells, periwinkles and even wild daffodils. He read me stories and was proud of my apparent prowess in reading, whereas, in fact, I knew the stories from memory having read them so many times.

We had a good relationship then, before I was old enough to question him or become the recipient of his sharp tongue. He was not physically violent in any way, and never even smacked me; but I was afraid of his quick temper. I shrivelled up at the unkindness of his words. In spite of this apparent harshness he was not an unfeeling man and I have more than once seen him near to tears over a distressing item of news. He was unable to show this emotional side in relation to me and seemed compelled to suppress his feelings.

My Father, William Price, by *Dilys Walter*.[42]

LETTER TO THE EDITOR FROM "DISGUSTED" OF CLIFTON

Salvation Army Collections. "A Major visited about 50 houses in wealthy Clifton and the result of his labours was **one shilling**!"

[I ask you! One shilling!!]

Clifton Chronicle, 1889.

And Another...

May I through your columns make a most decided and earnest protest against the commencement of Sunday omnibus traffic in this part of Clifton. Clifton has so long been famed for its quiet and orderly Sunday. Have the directors of the Omnibus Company no consideration for their horses or their men?

MAD SPEED IN CLIFTON

P.C. Roscow, who had been forced to jump out of the way when the car shot out at a junction, said he had been in the district for 15 years and he had never seen a car go so fast before. The defendant, Charles Henry Richards of 21, Pembroke Road, a well-known citizen, had been a motorist for 13 or 14 years. The car was built in 1907 and the older a car was, the more noise it made. "At no point was the car going at more than 10 or 12 mph," he said.

Fined £10 and 2gns costs. *Clifton Chronicle, 1913.*

But the old, staid Victorian life and the contrasting high spirits of the Edwardian era were about to come to an end. Devious and fumbling gropings for a military balance of power in Europe by politicians and royalty blew up in their faces with the assassination of the heir to the Austrian throne in Sarajevo in 1914; the old order fell apart and things would never be the same again. The lights went out all over Europe.

The First World War

About fifty-five thousand men from the Bristol area enlisted during the war. Around seven thousand of them died.(998 alone in the 1st Battalion of the Gloucestershire Regiment, not all Bristolians, of course.)

More than three thousand old boys from Clifton College enlisted. Between them they won a truly remarkable total of five VCs, 180 DSOs, and 300 MCs. Five hundred and eighty of them died, as did 137 men who had been to Bristol University; together, they won one VC, two DSOs, 42 MCs and one DFC.

At the peak of production two hundred flying machines were being produced at Filton, where from 1915-1917 there had been training squadrons of the Royal Flying Corps.

There was a remount depot at Shirehampton through which passed the astonishing total of 347,045 horses and mules, 317,165 of which had arrived from overseas. Bristol industry provided about everything you can think of for the war effort: planes, seaplanes, motor cycles, high explosives, boots, mustard gas and clothes, tobacco and chocolate.

A KHAKI WEDDING, 1916

Miss Mary Hunford Jones of Oakfield Road and Captain F. Birkett of the Queen's Royal West Surrey Regiment at Christchurch, Clifton. The bride's dress was of khaki honeycomb cloth trimmed with skink, nigger brown velvet hat trimmed with silk and veil to match and she carried a shower bouquet white carnations and lilies tied with the colours of The Queen's Regiment. The bridesmaids wore French gray cashmere.

The groom, who was educated at Monkton Combe School, joined his battalion in France in December 1914 and was slightly wounded in the arm. He rejoined and was dangerously wounded in both legs in May 1916, brought home and made a slow recovery.

Clifton Chronicle, January 1916.

Earl Haig

The most famous of Clifton College's old boys was Douglas Haig, who was to become a Field Marshal.

"Haig, Douglas, 1861-1928. Educated at Clifton College, Oxford University and Sandhurst. Commissioned into the 7th Hussars. Assigned to special service in the Sudan 1898. Staff officer to General Sir John French 1899. Became conspicuous for his ingenuity, enterprise and brilliant staff work. Was a column commander during the Boer War, 1900-02, then became Inspector General of Cavalry under General Lord Kitchener, 1903-06. Thence to a staff appointment in the War Office before taking over Aldershot District in 1911. Took command of the 1st Army Corps in the British Expeditionary Force in August 1914 and was noted for his "imperturbable calm" during the retreat from Mons. Became Commander-in-Chief of the British army in France, responsible for planning the Somme offensive in 1916. After the end of the Great War became Commander-in-Chief Home Forces in 1919, during which time he received the thanks of Parliament, a gift of £100,000 from the nation and was created an earl (1919). After leaving the active list as a Field Marshal he became President of the Royal British Legion, and instituted the Poppy Day Appeal which still bears his name today.

The Concise Dictionary of National Biography.

Another famous Cliftonian was AEJ Collins, a schoolboy who, in the summer of 1899 ensured an entry in Wisden when he scored 628 not out in a junior house match played on the north-east side of The Close. The page from the score book is treasured and accounts of the great innings can be found in newspapers of the day. Sadly, Collins died in 1915 in the Great War.

Flying High

The British and Colonial Aeroplane Company, founded by Sir George White, was registered in February 1910 with a nominal capital of £100. With the company established, two men were sent to Paris, where they arranged for a Zodiac biplane to be exhibited at the Olympia Air Show in London in March 1910. Afterwards, this aeroplane was taken to Brooklands, where it refused to fly. Within a few weeks a blatant copy was ready to fly, the first Bristol aircraft to leave the ground. It was called the Boxkite and some seventy-eight were built, at the rate of two a week.

Before the end of 1910 machines and men were on their way for demonstrations in India and Australia. At home two aircraft were loaned to the War Office for the annual Army exercises on Salisbury Plain, one for the Red Force, the other for the Blue. (Some generals saw no point in having exercises at all if both sides could so quickly learn what the other side was doing!) However the War Minister was persuaded to form an Army Air Battalion and four Boxkites were ordered. Word reached Russia, and their order was for eight.

"On Saturday, the Bristol biplane was taken out for a ten minutes' trip. The whirring of the propeller, a short, swift run, and the aeroplane rose gracefully in the air, speeding forward at a height of about thirty feet ... the maximum height reached was about 100 feet. During the afternoon, thousands assembled on the Downs. At 2.45 p.m. Sir George White ordered another flight and amidst ringing cheers M. Tetard, the famous French aviator, took his seat upon the biplane and circled the Downs. It was evident to the spectators that during a large part of the flight the aeroplane was badly buffeted by the wind, and it speaks volumes for the skill of M. Tetard and the quality of the biplane that he was able to give so fine an exhibition under such adverse weather conditions. Nevertheless, he landed lightly as a bird in a space kept clear by the police."

The Bristol Times and Mirror, November, **1910**.

And, Two Months Later...

"The Boxkite of 1910 was a mass of light spars, piano wire and fabric which responded to every change of temperature; and as the nights were very cold with a heavy dew while the sun by day was burning hot, we found ourselves up against all sorts of difficulties in rigging. The spars bowed, the wires stretched and contracted, the fabric sagged, the whole structure creaked and cracked as if it were going to fall to pieces. We mounted the engine, a 50 hp Gnome, but owing to faulty rigging we broke two struts in the box-shaped tail when running it up. Then we found that the petrol provided was of inferior quality and had to telegraph for fresh supplies. But in spite of everything we were ready in time to make a trial flight the afternoon before the manoeuvres started.

These manoeuvres involved the concentration of four cavalry brigades and one infantry brigade, so we had a great crowd to see our maiden effort - a crowd which included twelve British Generals! Rumours had gone round the countryside that someone was going to fly; thousands of the local inhabitants came in from all sides and camped along the railway in order to see this latest madness of the sahib. Since Hindu religion definitely recognises the possibility of flying, these simple peasants were not nearly so incredulous as our own villagers would have been.

The Boxkite of that day was not a particularly comfortable conveyance. The pilot sat on the leading edge of the lower plane with his feet on a rudder bar which was supported by an outrigger through which he looked down between his knees into space. The observer sat close behind and somewhat higher than the pilot with his legs round the latter's body, and he also had a direct view down. Our only instruments were an oil-pulsating gauge which didn't work, and an aneroid barometer, which I think I wore round my neck.

I must admit that by the time we had the engine running and were taxi-ing across our improved aerodrome followed by an immense cloud of dust I was thoroughly frightened but as we rose gently and swiftly from the ground I experienced one of the most glorious moments of my life - one of my most precious dreams had come true! For this was my first flight - January 1911.

We climbed to one thousand feet and flew round for half an hour. Within a few minutes I was thoroughly enjoying myself watching the local inhabitants, cattle and poultry stampeding in every direction. We then made a perfect landing and, full of glorious exhilaration, set to work to prepare for our first reconnaissance. I received a sealed envelope from Sir Douglas Haig containing orders for the following day.

The troops at Aurangabad were supposed to be an advanced guard moving south who had lost touch with a hostile force which was retreating through Jalna. Our job was to locate the retiring force and bring back information regarding its strength and dispositions; our own cavalry had not yet got into touch with the retreating enemy. We started soon after six a.m. It was a glorious Indian cold weather morning; the air was like champagne and as clear as crystal. Before we had been in the air ten minutes, I saw heavy clouds of dust away to the south, and pointed them out triumphantly to Jullerot. We headed for them at eleven hundred feet, which was pretty near the ceiling of our old Boxkite. We flew over them for about ten minutes, during which time I located every company and section of the rear-guard, and recorded them on the drawing block. So good was the visibility that I could almost recognise a friend of mine whom I knew was commanding the Horse Artillery. We then flew home, only to find our landing-place occupied by a raiding party of hostile cavalry. However, we got down a little further on, and under cover of a native hut I made out my report."

And Twenty-Eight Years After That...

It was a Bristol Blenheim which was first over the line in the Second World War. Two days before war was declared, Blenheim crews had been standing by at Wyton to reconnoitre and photograph German naval bases. Within forty-eight minutes of Chamberlain's broadcast, a Blenheim piloted by Flying Officer A. McPherson, carrying a naval observer, was on its way across the German frontier. Enemy warships were seen emerging from Wilhelmshaven. The performance of the aircraft cheated the incident of its value; they flew at 24,000 feet and the intense cold put the radio out of action: consequently they could not report till they returned to base. By that time the afternoon was already turning to evening. Thunderstorms and darkness prevented the Blenheim striking force from taking off on the first evening of the war, September 3rd. [33]

The Bristol Engineering Company, makers of aero engines, had built 17,000 piston engines which powered many types of Bristol aircraft before they began the construction of jet engines. In 1960 they built the Pegasus engine that powers the highly successful vertical take-off Harrier, used by the Royal Air Force, the Royal Navy and the US Marine Corps. They also created the Olympus engines that power Concorde. The company was merged with Rolls Royce of Derby in 1976.

These aeronauts were following in the footsteps of

George Pocock, a 19th Century St. Michael's schoolmaster, took to kite-flying on a grand scale, building enormous kites and harnessing them to a "Kite Carriage". Loaded with six passengers it was often to be seen trundling across the Downs at up to 25 m.p.h.

For years Pocock and his family travelled all around Bristol by kite carriage, much to the annoyance of toll gate keepers since kite-powered transport was immune from tolls. As time went by he created kites so large that they could pull four carriages at once. He also cruised the Bristol Channel in a kite yacht.

Another inventor was...

WILLIAM FRIESE-GREENE, who was born at 69, College Street, Bristol on the 7th September 1855 and became a pupil at Queen Elizabeth's Hospital School.

By a grant from the Patent Office of Patent No. I0131 dated 2Ist June 1889 for a Camera and Projector using perforated celluloid films for taking and projecting moving pictures Friese-Greene, then aged 35, in effect became the inventor of Cinematography.

He had a long dispute with Thomas Edison, who had claimed that he invented the new process, but in the end an American Court found in Friese-Greene's favour.

Bristol Trams

I have in mind a man whose picture has stayed in my memory for many years. In the old days of tram travel, when the stinging snowflakes swept into the driver's platform, it looked as though only two pink and very damp eyes were seeing the tram along, despite the fact that its inside was crammed with sitting and standing passengers.

The rest of the driver's person was wrapped well against the cold weather. A sou-wester covered his face and ears, a muffler was wound around his throat and a long rubber Macintosh protected his body, reaching down to the top of wellington boots. Even his hands had on them something warm and waterproof.

How different from summer's days, when drivers wore a thin white dust coat, and a peaked cap with a top covering of white to reflect the sun.(37)

Bristol Buses

Bristol's first motor bus service, between the Victoria Rooms and the Clifton Suspension Bridge, began at 7·50 a.m. on 17th January 1906, and ran every 10 minutes until 11 p.m. The fare was 1d. Little public excitement was reported at the time, but the service was soon followed on February 5th by services from Horfield tram terminus to Thornbury, from Brislington tram terminus to Saltford, and from Hanham tram terminus to Kelston, with a further service starting on February 8th between Redland and Westbury.

By Easter Monday of 1906 12 motor-buses were in service, with three surviving horse-buses in addition. In that year the company carried 46,902,257 passengers.(38)

Forty-seven million, for Pete's sake!!

[These days they nearly all go by car, as we know only too well.]

St Philips in the 1920s

When Blake wrote of those 'dark satanic mills' he aptly described St. Philips, a place with a saintly name but deathly surroundings. It was **six square miles of manure works, gas works, corporation refuse tips, knackers yards, rag and bone works and soap works.** It also included a firm making sausages and pork pies and a factory making custard. It was a residential district for 50,000 rats, 100,000 bugs, and in the summer a resort for a million flies attracted there by the Feeder Canal into which spewed all the industrial waste of industry and also the River Avon, a tidal river flowing to and fro like a huge lavatory flush, taking away all the human waste which was deposited on the mud banks until the tide would roll back to collect more effluent for transmission into the sea adjacent to the seaside resorts of Clevedon and Weston Super Mare. Besides the extensive rodent and vermin population there also lived ten thousand humans; men, women and children. Danny *Price*[42]

The Church Cat

Alfred Hollins, who had been blind from birth, was for many years organist at St. George's Church, Edinburgh. In his memoirs he wrote :

"Morgan (Ralph Morgan, organist at St. Mary Redcliffe during the 1920s and 1930s) and I used to go into the church about seven, and we often stayed till after ten, taking it in turns to play to each other. One night we found a black pussy waiting for us. Morgan told me that she had come to the church ever since he had been a there, and that she was a very musical pussy, always waiting for him when he went to practise, ready to follow him in to church and, as soon as he got settled at the organ, jump on to his knee and sit quietly the whole time. Realising that I was a stranger, instead of sitting on my knee she sat beside me on the organ stool. I used often to leave off playing in order to stroke her.

She lived in the church for nearly fifteen years, and her grave in the churchyard is marked with a neat little stone inscribed: "The Church cat".[39]

Harveys of Bristol

William Perry, who founded the famous wine merchants at the end of the 18th Century, lived in Park Street, next door to Thomas Harvey, a sea captain. During the early-19th Century , when the world-famous Bristol Cream was first blended, a member of the Harvey family married a Perry. The Harvey family eventually took over and expanded the business, based in Denmark Street. Some of the vaults in which the port and sherry were stored were originally part of the 13th Century Gaunt's Hospital, which became the Lord Mayor's Chapel. In modern times they have been converted into a wine museum and a fine restaurant.

Harveys were taken over by Showering, the cider company, in 1966, and presently are part of the Allied Domecq Group, with offices in The Pavilions, on the airport road.

Eddy Harvey, Chairman 1919-1937

In his younger days Eddy was a stickler for neatness in handwriting, and set the office junior, whom he considered lacking in this virtue, to copy his own hand - than which, at least in his own opinion, there could be no better model. The young man complied, and improved so much that nearly forty years later the Chairman complimented him on his writing. He was duly grateful, and reminded the Chief of his advice, which he had long since forgotten. "Well, well," said the old gentleman. "That must account for my overdraft."

Eddy spent much of his spare time in his workshop and garden, and often on Saturday afternoons in summer two of the warehousemen were invited to his home as helpers. They generally accepted with pleasure, for the old gentleman was kind and generous, and there were many incidents which on Monday morning filled the cellars with laughter.

One Saturday the task was to water the flower beds. Water was fetched from a well some half-mile from the house in a milk churn mounted on a crank-axle cart which was drawn by a donkey. With due ceremony the turn-out and its driver set off; but it failed to return. The Chairman, looking across the fields, saw the donkey rooted to the ground and the unfortunate driver doing everything he could to persuade it to move, but without avail. The man pulled, pushed and beat, but the animal refused to budge. The Chairman knew a better way. He walked across, lifted the donkey's ear and shouted into it one word: "Home!" At once it set off at such a pace that the two elderly men came panting behind.

But as well as being a character, Eddy Harvey had a serious and kindly nature, as this story demonstrates. An employee was found in a state of acute depression because he had furnished his home on the hire purchase system and could not pay the instalments. The extent of the debt turned out to be £40. Eddy made out a cheque for that amount, then asked the man's permission to take two shillings a week from his wages for repayment. When Christmas time came there was no Christmas box for that man. It was a sore disappointment, until he was told that his outstanding debt to the firm - £39, allowing for the weekly payments - had been forgiven.(40)

Colston's Girls' School

The continued existence of one of Bristol's long established girls' independent schools [1891], Colston's Girls' School, is due to the resourcefulness and initiative of a group of sailors.

On the night of Good Friday **1941** when Bristol was raided by the German air force the School Hall was saved from fire by the sailors of H M Training Ship *'Cabot'* who were lodged there. It would be interesting to know how many of the sailors who saved the school are in fact still living in Bristol. Whoever they are, they will be pleased to know that fifty-four years later, the school flourishes.

JP Franklin,
Head Mistress, 1995

The Second World War

Things began quietly. On the 18th June 1940 a single bomber attacked the Bristol Aircraft Works at Filton. On 3rd July Whittocks End was bombed; casualties were one pig, five ducks, two rabbits and a hay rick.

However, on 22nd-23rd August more than 400 bombs fell on Filton and the neighbouring villages; the aircraft factory was severely damaged. On the 21st September more than 60 bombers raided Bristol, dropping 300 bombs; Filton aircraft works was hit by 160 bombs, six of which fell directly on shelters. Hundreds of people were killed or injured. Eight enemy planes were shot down or crashed. On 27th September ninety German bombers and fighters attacked but were driven off in a memorable air fight over the city. Seven enemy planes were downed. On 2nd November more than 5,000 incendiaries and 10,000 high explosive bombs rained down; more than 200 people died, 700 were injured and 10,000 houses were damaged or destroyed. Many historic buildings were ruined. The Germans boasted that Bristol had been destroyed.

BUT It took just one night for the history of centuries to vanish in flames and rubble. Sunday, 24th November 1940 was the night that the war came to Bristol, and when that terrible night was over, little remained of some of Bristol's favourite buildings and streets. "The City of Churches had in one night become the city of ruins," wrote the Lord Mayor, Alderman Thomas Underwood in an account of the blitz, written in 1942. "In the most heavily bombed area, entire streets were completely devastated whilst in other streets wide gaping wounds showed isolated premises which had miraculously escaped destruction.

"Wine Street, held by many to be the most valuable shopping street in the provinces, was reduced to a mass of rubble. Castle Street, built on the site of Bristol's Norman castle precincts, suffered almost as completely.

"Severely damaged shopping streets in other districts were College Green, Park Street, Queen's Road, Redcliff Street, Thomas Street and Victoria Street. Many historic buildings and architectural treasures were destroyed."

They included St Peter's Hospital, a medieval building which had been home to alchemists and pirates, and housed the Royal Mint and Britain's first sugar refinery. The old Dutch House, a beautiful black and white half-timbered house, went, as did the city museum, the art gallery, much of the university - including the beautiful Great Hall - the Prince's Theatre, the Upper Arcade shops, three churches dating back to Norman times, seven modern ones, eight schools, alms-houses, cinemas, Georgian houses, and factories. Ten thousand homes were also damaged or destroyed.

The attack had begun at 6.50 pm with flares falling from the skies. Then the bombers arrived. "Showers of incendiary bombs kindled and spread the conflagration," wrote Alderman Underwood. "High-explosive bombs whistled and screamed to earth. Many were of extremely large calibre and spread the raging fires from building to building until whole streets were ablaze.

"The flames appeared as one huge fiery furnace leaping high into the air and giving an intensity of daylight over a great part of the city."[41]

On 3rd January 1941, in a new blitz, planes dropped 10,000 incendiaries. On 4th January 7,000 incendiaries fell on Avonmouth. On 16th here was an 11-hour blitz on Bristol and Avonmouth. On 11th and 12th April, during what were called the Good Friday Raids, after incendiaries earlier in the day the city was attacked by more than 150 bombers. Again, there was appalling damage, particularly in the central area of the city and in Knowle, Hotwells, and Filton. 180 people died, 381 were injured. 6,500 AA shells were fired in defence of the city.

25th April was the date of the last major blitz, which hit Bedminster, Brislington and Knowle. Sixteen people were killed, 28 were injured and 1,200 houses were damaged.

*

PANIC

"The morning of the 12th of April 1941 was freezing cold, with snow on the Ground, pitch black. The Night Watchman gave me a strange look when I arrived and started work. Expecting to find Mother and Ginger the cat on one of the floors after a while I asked the Watchman where mother was? I froze when he said, 'Haven't you heard, son? Your home was bombed last night!'

"I flew, running, sobbing and praying all at the same time. As I turned the corner what a dreadful sight greeted me as it was beginning to get light. The bomb had struck the top floor of the house at the rear - ploughing its way downwards bringing the three floors down to the front garden. The roof was almost intact. I nearly went crazy thinking of Mother, Doreen and Eileen buried under all that rubble or debris. I started clawing at the rubble begging the Air Raid Wardens to help me. They calmed me down, then I noticed Bill the lodger lying dead on the grass. The men told me that a woman had been taken to the B.R.I. I ran all the way to the Infirmary, where injured people were everywhere, but they had no one brought in by our name. In desperation as no buses seemed to be running I spent the rest of the day in a daze cadging lifts from cars or lorries to the General Hospital, out to Southmead and every hospital I could think of, convinced that Mother, Doreen and Eileen were all buried alive in that house, it never occurred to me to phone around all these different hospitals as I was in such a state.

"I can't remember much else about that day except why, I don't know, I went back to the B.R.I at 6 pm and mentioned Bill the lodger's surname and there sure enough was poor Mother tucked away in the corner of the ward, still covered in dirt and dust with serious head Injuries. She had been buried for thirteen hours under 16 ft of debris, she was barely conscious but was able to put my mind at rest. Doreen and Eileen were alive and well having stayed the night with relations when the Raid started. Apparently the rescue men had heard Mother's cries and hoping she would not lose consciousness, having her voice as a guide to her whereabouts, had said in broad Bristol accents, 'all right, my love, we'll take thee for a drink when we gets thee out. '"

I hope those brave men never found out that it was their shovels that caused poor Mother's head injuries. It may have worried them all their lives if they had known that she was to die in six months. No one could possibly blame them for doing their duty. All I could think of at the time was that Mum was alive and after we found a home somewhere possibly all the family could get back together again?

Five people were killed in that house that night, Bill and the Banker's family, by some miracle the little baby was thrown clear and uninjured, so now forty four years later, he or she may be married with a family of their own? Life goes on. **Ron Glade** (42)

A total of 1,299 Bristolians were killed by bombs and 3,305 were injured during 78 air raids.

Rt Hon Tony Benn, M.P.

Privy Councillor 1964. RAFVR 1943-45, RNVR 1945-46. Represented Bristol South-East **1950-60,** and **1963-83**. Postmaster General 1964-66, Minister for Technology 1966-70, Minister for Aviation 1967, for Power 1969, for Industry and Post & Telecommunications 1974-75, for Energy 1975-79.

And here are some of the things he has said:

"I am on the right wing of the middle of the road with a strong radical bias."
Dictionary of 20th Century Quotations, ed. Nigel Rees

"The British House of Lords is the British Outer Mongolia for retired politicians."
(*On renouncing his peerage. **The Observer**, 4th February, 1962.*

"A faith is something you die for; a doctrine is something you kill for: there is all the difference in the world."
The Observer, Sayings of the Week, 16th April 1989.

Another Great Storm

Wednesday 10th July **1968** - Disaster Day

Heavy rain had been falling for most of the day and by mid-evening thunder and lightning had reached torrential proportions in Bristol and North Somerset. It was the worst rainstorm to hit the area in over half a century, with more than five inches of rain falling in less than 24 hours.

The full fury of the flood was felt during the hours of darkness. By 5am almost every stream, brook and river in the area had burst its banks, causing death, devastation and despair on a scale greater than any in living memory. That night, seven people lost their lives, hundreds more suffered a terrifying ordeal of hardship and loss, bridges that had stood for centuries were swept away or were severely damaged, as were countless houses, shops, factories and other properties. Most street lights were out and a number of cars were washed off the Bath Hill bridge. Some low-lying properties were flooded to a depth of 14 feet and several residents had to seek refuge in attics or on roofs when the water swept into first-floor bedrooms. Several people reported seeing manhole covers balanced on spouts of water in the road.

At 6, Hollywood Road Mrs Elizabeth Bastin was having her supper when she felt the carpet move beneath her feet - it was water coming up through the floor! Mrs Bastin later said that seconds after that all the doors burst in and she was up to her shoulders in water. She managed to get into her kitchen and climb on to the gas stove, which was the only thing not floating away! Her cries for help were heard by brothers Michael and Richard Sweet, Mr Stephen Harris and PC Wayne Butcher. To get to her, they had to move a massive pile of furniture and break down the kitchen door - all this in a chest-high raging torrent of water that was rushing in through the front door of the house and out the back.

147

At Stockwood Vale, where some people were trapped, the water was already three feet deep and rising rapidly. Guided by cries for help, Firemen Burford and Hembrow and a Police Constable were eventually able to reach a stranded van. The occupants, two men and a lady, were rescued and taken to safety via a tortuous route which included stumbling through a ploughed field, wading through chest-high water and climbing a garden wall - all in torrential rain and near darkness.

By 1.00 am what had been severe flooding had become a disaster. A number of eye witnesses described a "wall of water," a "tidal wave" rushing down the Chew valley. A Ford Zephyr car and its four occupants were washed off the Bath Hill Bridge. Three of them were drowned. Staff at Keynsham Hospital had to deal with several maternity cases without either water or electricity; the Police rushed water supplies to them.

At Dapps Hill, several cottages and the general stores owned by Mr & Mrs Bill Brewer were awash. Mr Brewer lost his entire collection of forty racing pigeons. Nearby, Mr & Mrs Cole, their three daughters and son and Mrs Cole's mother were forced to spend the night in the attic as the water reached a depth of almost four feet in their upstairs bedrooms. In the early hours a special constable engaged in rescue work on a roof-top noticed submerged street lights still shining under the water. At the bottom of Harptree Hill, underground pressure caused by the volume of water rushing down from the Mendips forced holes through the road and caused waterspouts over six feet high.

The 10.05pm double decker bus from Bristol to Bath with 18 passengers on board reached Brislington at 10.25pm and became marooned in about 3 feet of raging water in Brislington Square. The water was rising rapidly and by 11.00pm had reached 7 feet deep. The passengers were rescued by two boats, one a Fire Service inflatable, the other a private dinghy, just after midnight. The water was so deep that the occupants of the bus had no difficulty in stepping from the top deck emergency door into the boats. (43)

The Bristol Tapestry

There are 27 main panels in it, each 18 inches high and about 18 inches wide, though some large scenes spread over two or even three panels. There are 5,000 letters, using 300 skeins. Mrs Lily Walker, aged 81 did much valuable work on the first section. The youngest needlewoman was nine-year old Katie Nichols, while the oldest was Mrs Laura Hunt, a lady of 85.

During the 600th anniversary celebrations of the granting of the charter to Bristol the tapestry was displayed on the Downs. The Queen and Prince Philip were to inspect the Tapestry on 9th August **1973**. 4th August was wild, wet and windy and Sunday 5th brought strong winds and torrential rains. It was little consolation to the ladies that their work was insured for £5,000, for it was beyond price and could never be replaced.

Gales howled all night and by five o'clock in the morning the tent was wrecked, trailing the labours of four years on the rain-sodden ground. Orange and blue dye from the tent canvas mingled with mud stains. The beautiful original paintings and drawings which had been on view as well were torn, trampled, bedraggled. The Committee cut the tapestry free and it was taken to the City Museum's Conservation Department. Luckily, linen is one of the more durable textiles and all the materials used were of good quality. Mr. Wheeler, husband of one of the seamstresses, made a frame on which it was stretched to help re-shape and strain the cloth. It had to remain on the stretcher for almost three years but the results were good.

On 9th August, the finished section, looking much refreshed, hung in the entrance hall of the City Museum. The unfinished portions, ranged on long tables in front of it, were being worked on by the four committee members, who had the honour of being Presented to Her Majesty and the Duke of Edinburgh while the rest of those associated with the project watched from the balcony above.[44]

[The Tapestry is now housed in Baker's Hall, Quaker's Friars, where it may be seen by appointment and during an open day in September.]

My St Paul's

A black bag, was a safety passport to anywhere at any time. But there was one night of terror to remember in St. Pauls.

Delivery by gaslight was not ideal, having been used to all mod cons in hospital labour wards. This particular middle of the night things were coming along very well. Citizen 1944 had delivered himself as far as the eyebrows when the gaslight gave a despairing dip and expired!

"Don't push. Strike a match. Get a candle. Turn off the gas tap.

Somebody DO something." (I couldn't do anything but hang on.)

Mother pushed. The head was out.

"Please God, don't let the cord be around the neck." It wasn't.

"Please God, let the shoulders rotate." They did.

"Please don't let them stick." They didn't.

Nature took over.

The infant yelled, so I had not let it drown.

The mother contracted, so I had not let her bleed to death.

After an aeon of eternity's, a match was struck, and a stump of candle produced. It might have been a tiny flickering flame to the Universe, but it was a beacon of salvation to me... and a warning. I managed to scrounge a couple of inches of candle and a few matches, and made sure I always had a few coins for meter feeding until I could afford to buy a torch. (My salary worked out at a bit less than £5 a month at the time.) *E.L.L.Shaddick* (42)

As I went out one evening,
Walking down Bristol Street,
The crowds upon the pavement
Were fields of harvest wheat.

And down by the brimming river
I heard a lover sing
Under the arch of a railway:
"Love it has no ending;

I'll love you, dear, I'll love you
Till China and Africa meet,
And the river jumps over the mountain
And salmon sing in the street.

I'll love you till the ocean
Is folded up and dry,
And the seven stars go squawking
Like geese about the sky.

The years shall run like rabbits,
For in my arms I hold
The Flower of the Ages,
And the first love of the world."

But all the clocks of the city
Began to whirr and chime:
"O let not Time deceive you,
You cannot conquer Time.

In the burrows of the Nightmare
Where justice naked is,
Time watches from the shadows
And coughs when you would kiss.

In headaches and in worry,
Vaguely life leaks away,
And Time will have his fancy
Tomorrow or today.

Into many a green valley
Drifts the appalling snow,
Time breaks the threaded dances
And the diver's brilliant bow.

O plunge your hands in water,
Plunge them in up to the wrist;
Stare, stare in the basin
And wonder what you've missed.

The glacier knocks in the cupboard,
The desert sighs in the bed,
And the crack in the teacup opens
A lane to the land of the dead.

Where the beggars raffle banknotes
And the giant is enchanting to Jack,
And the lily-white boy is a roarer,
And Gill goes down on her back.

O look, look in the mirror,
O look in your distress;
Life remains a blessing
Although you cannot bless.

O stand, stand at the window
As the tears scald and start;
"You'll love your crooked neighbour
With all your crooked heart."

It was late, late in the evening,
The lovers they were gone;
The clocks had ceased their chiming
And the deep river ran on.

W.H. Auden
[Beautiful, isn't it?]

151

Something else to be Proud Of

The Gloucestershire Regiment, the Glorious Glosters, who earned that name, and the right to wear the American Presidential Unit citation on their uniform, for their epic stand on the Imjin River during the Korean War in the early Nineteen-Fifties. The regiment has the Freedom of the City. It has now merged with other infantry regiments and become the Royal Gloucestershire, Berkshire and Wiltshire Regiment.

.....and too, of course there are the

Royal Marines Reserve, whose West Country base is at Dorset House in Clifton

.....and, not least, the senior service, the

There have been seven Ships of the Line named H.M.S. Bristol, the first of them launched three hundred and fifty years ago. The latest was the guided missile destroyer now decommissioned and used in Portsmouth as an accommodation ship for sea cadets. In 1982 it was part of the South Atlantic Task Force in the Falklands War.

There are a total of some 4,000 personnel in the Royal Naval Reserve, roughly one tenth of the Royal Navy's peacetime strength. Sailors of the Royal Naval Reserve from Bristol and the surrounding towns, men and women, train at HMS Flying Fox, on Winterstoke Road - where members of the Shakespeare Club meet once a month, by courtesy of the Commanding Officer. The club was formed in 1955. Its first meetings were held in the Skakespeare pub in Victoria Street in the city centre, hence the name. Presently there are over seventy Shakespeareans, nearly all of them retired officers of the armed forces. Which leads us on, naturally enough, to...

Those over 60...

who preceded frozen foods, yoghurt and instant coffee; plastics, contact lenses, frisbees and The Pill. They arrived on the scene before radar, laser beams, credit cards and ballpoint pens; before dishwashers, tumble dryers, electric blankets, air conditioners, drip-dry clothes and disposable nappies. Before atoms had been split and long before man first walked on the moon. Before FM radio, videos, tape decks, computers, word processors and artificial hearts.

They thought 'fast food' was what you ate during Lent, a 'Big Mac' was a large raincoat, and 'crumpet' was something you had for tea. Sheltered accommodation' was where you waited for a bus. A 'chip' was a piece of wood, 'hardware' meant nuts and bolts, and software wasn't even in the dictionary. 'Making out' referred to how well people did in their exams, a 'stud' was something that fastened a collar to a shirt, and 'going all the way' meant staying on the bus as far as the depot! 'Coke' was kept in the coalhole, a 'joint' was a piece of meat eaten on Sundays, and 'grass' was mown. A pot was something food was cooked in. 'Rock music' was a lullaby, a 'gay' person was the life and soul of the party, and 'aids' were cosmetics women put on their faces to make themselves look prettier. Young men didn't have long hair and wear earrings, let alone nose rings. People usually married first, *then* lived together (how square could you get?). *ANON*

How the world has changed!

And don't forget

Where would we be without them?

And, finally, an Epilogue

in which there's a moral for us all

23rd January 1826. I dined yesterday with Kearsey, a man wallowing in the comforts of life and luxuries, and from ill health in consequence of too great a relish for them, rendered totally insensible and indifferent to their value or their enjoyment. There he lay, on a down sofa, with a Turkey carpet, a roaring fire, a beautiful garden, a nice house, a copious dinner, rich wines, tarts, confectionery, a carriage, horses, servants, & money, blasting everything, cursing the garden, damning the frost, sneering at his cabbages, ridiculing the soil of his ground, groaning over his hay, scolding his wife, abusing his nephews, and saying was there not another world, he had not been fairly used in this! - and why? Because he, being too fond of eating, had by an improper indulgence, brought on a diseased vision, which rendered his life a burthen.

"Christ Jesus, Lord Jesus, God Almighty," said he, as he lay surrounded with comforts, "what I suffer!"

Benjamin Robert Haydon, Diary, 1857

SOURCES REFERRED TO IN THE TEXT
To whom grateful thanks are extended for the use of the excerpts.

1. **Bristol, England**, H.G. Brown & P.J. Harris, The Burleigh Press, Bristol 1946

2. **Bristol Week End**, 11th May 1962

3. **Bristol**, Harold G Brown, Rankin Bros, Bristol 1946

4. **Leading Events in the History of the port of Bristol**, WN Reid & WE Hicks, The Western Daily Press, 1877

5. **Bristol**, Tudor Edwards, Batsford, London 1951

6. **The Story of Old Bristol**, E.M.Hapgood, Printed by Dolphin Publicity 1966

7. **St Mark's Chapel**, Elizabeth Ralph & Henley Evans, Bristol Corporation,1979

8. **A History of Bristol**, the Rev John Evans, W Sheppard, Bristol 1816

9. **"Bristolia: A Poem"**, 600 years of Bristol Poetry (Bristol, 1973)

10. **Accounts of the Constables of Bristol Castle**, Margaret Sharp, Bristol Record Society 1982

11. **The Widening Gate**, David Harris Stacks, University of California Press, Oxford, England 1991

12. **The Columbus Myth**, Ian Wilson, Simon & Schuster, London, 1991

13. **This is Bristol**, John Trelawny-Ross & Bryan Little, Redcliffe Press, Bristol, 1982

14. **Calendar of the Bristol Apprentice Book**, Bristol Record Society, 1980

15. **Bristol's Earliest Photographs**, Reece Winstone, Bristol

16. **Bristol and its Municipal Government 1820-1851**, Bristol Record Society's publications, Volume XXIX 1976

17. **Bristol, Africa and the 18th Century slave trade to America**, David Richardson, Bristol Record Society 1986

18. **The City and County of Bristol**, Bryan Little, Werner Laurie, London, 1954

19. **Smuggling in the Bristol Channel, 1700-1850**, Graham Smith, Countryside Books 1989

20. **Bristol First**, The first Bristol to London mail coach run, Bevan Rider, for the Bristol & West Building Society 1984.

21. **The Bristol Old Vic, the First Ten Years**, by Audrey Williamson & Charles Langstone, Garnet Miller Ltd, London 1957

22. **A West Country Doctor**, Colin Wintle 1982

23. **The Civil War Defences of Bristol**, James Russell 1995

24. **Bristol Mirror**, 13th Sep 1806

25. **Frenchay Church of England School**, Carol Thorne, Bristol 1992

26. **Industrial Archaeology of the Bristol Region**, by A. Buchanan & Neil Cossons, David & Charles, Newton Abbott 1969

27. **"Bristol Worthies"** AB Freeman, Burleigh Ltd, Bristol 1909

28. **Portrait of Bristol** by Keith Brace, Robert Hale, London 1971

29. **Famous Bristolians**, David Foot, Redcliffe Press 1979

30. **Hotheads & Heroes**, Peter Macdonald, Christopher Davies, Swansea 1987

31. **The Nailsea Glassworks**, , HG & MA Thomas, 1987

32. **Clifton School Days 1879-1885**, O.F. Christie, Shaylor, London 1930

33. **Bristol Fashion**, John Pudney, Putnam, London 1960

34. **Shipwrecks of the Bristol Channel**, Graham Smith, Countryside Books, Newbury, 1991

35. **Portrait of a Zoo**, Robert & Anne Warren, Redcliffe Press, Bristol 1985

36. **'A Holiday Fete At The Zoo Gardens, Clifton, August 8, 1893,'** from the Diary of a Bristolian, by W.H. Bow.

37. **Bristol Reflections**, Gilbert Croker, Bristol Broadsides (Co-0p) Ltd, Bristol 1988

38. **Bristol's Buses**, P.Hulin

39. **Bristol Curiosities**, Reece Winston & Glynn Duggan, The Redcliffe Press 1979

40. **Bristol Cream**, Godfrey Harrison, Batsford Ltd, London 1955

41. **Bristol Evening Post**, "Victory" Souvenir Supplement, Bristol, 1995

42. **Bristol Lives**, Ron Glade, A Bristol Broadsides book 1987

43. **Bristol, The Great Flood of '68**, by Terry Staples

44. **Bristol: One thousand years in Stitches**, Kathleen Philpott, Bristol, 1991

Picture credits: Bristol City Council: Pages 2, 11, 15, 32, 35, 36, 37, 38, 76, 78, 79, 84, 86, 112, 113, 114, 116 (top).

Bristol Evening Post: Pages 10, 39, 40, 71, 77, 110, 111, 116 (bottom) and front cover picture.

The author wishes to acknowledge with thanks the assistance given by Bristol City Council and Bristol Evening Post.

This book may be ordered by post through J.W. Arrowsmith Ltd, Winterstoke Road, Bristol BS3 2NT or by phoning 0117 9667545, (fax 0117 9637829) or on e-mail address Petmac@Delphi.com

Peter Macdonald was in the British Army for more than thirty years. He was City Swordbearer and Lord Mayor's Secretary in the early 1980s before concentrating on writing. He has had the following books published

FICTION

The Hope of Glory
Wide Horizons
Exit
One Way Street
Dead End

NON-FICTION

Stopping the Clock:
Bomb disposal in the world of terrorism

Hotheads and Heroes:
The Bristol Riots of 1831

Minutes of Time:
A World History

Giap:
The Victor in Vietnam